650
S0-BBO-739

LIKE MOONLIGHT ON SNOW

LIKE MOONLIGHT ON SNOW

The Life of Simon Iturri Patiño

by JOHN HEWLETT

Illustrated

ROBERT M. McBRIDE & COMPANY
New York

PRINTED IN THE UNITED STATES OF AMERICA

FIRST EDITION

AMERICAN BOOK–STRATFORD PRESS, INC., NEW YORK

TO JEANNE

Contents

Illustrations

1

Legend of the Andes

Simon Iturri Patiño, the tin king of Bolivia, is one of the world's mysterious figures, a fabulous, Buddha-faced little half-breed who has become more of a legend than a man. The world's inhabitants know little or nothing about him, yet there is scarcely one of them whose life has not been affected by Patiño's existence, not even the primitive tribesman in the African jungle, nor the Jivaro head-hunter of Ecuador. The firing of a gun anywhere, at any time, adds to his already incredible fortune; the death of a human being increases his wealth; a housewife who opens a can of soup makes him richer.

The sources of Patiño's wealth and power lie precisely in such simple, homely acts—the snap of an electric light switch, the buying of a pair of spectacles, a blind man holding out his cup, the tolling of church bells. All things flow from Patiño: beds and bar rails, telephones and loudspeakers, limousines and tractors, radios and surgical instruments. And from the multitudinous use of these articles, wealth flows back to Patiño.

The portrait of such a man requires a mixture of exotic pigments. There must be the subtle shading of Zaharoff, the bold stroke of Krueger, the broad pattern of Rothschild, a golden dash of Midas, and a pathetic touch of Pagliacci. In the end, it is a picture that no one sees clearly, for Patiño's life has been made up of distortions, contradictions and sheer magic.

Consequently there are many Patiños. There is the Patiño who appears to his enemies as ruthless, sinister; an exploiter, a warmonger, an intriguer and a shedder of other men's blood. This Patiño is a man who uses his immense wealth and power to move nations into positions of monopoly, who employs international banking to control world figures and world resources.

But there is also the Patiño who is known to his friends and associates as the greatest man of high purpose on the globe, a friend of kings, a *bon vivant* celebrated in every capital, a man known and respected by financiers, potentates, munitions czars and dictators. Yet he is the same Patiño who is called by his enemies "the octopus of the Andes."

It is true that the world owes him something, no matter what kind of man he may be. Because of Patiño's tin, scientists are able to use their microscopes in research; airplanes fly, telegrams and cables are sent, and even the decorations on Christmas trees are made possible. The type which prints these words is partly due to Patiño. From the base of his mighty empire, he has the most complete hold on daily human needs of any man in world history.

The core of it all is the silvery base metal ore from which comes tin. It is an ore that has the serene beauty of moonlight on snow.

Through his control of an essential metal, Patiño has lifted himself from an almost unimaginable poverty to an equally unimaginable wealth. He began life as a penniless, Spanish-Indian *cholo,* one of the lowliest inhabitants of land-locked Bolivia. Once he possessed $250, all his savings, but sudden calamity made him penniless again. At that moment he had only the rough clothes on his back and the confidence of a neighbor who loaned him an undersized mule so that he could make a heartbreaking climb into the basement of the stratosphere. There he found the wealth that transformed him from impoverished prospector to Midas.

Some North Americans have compared Patiño's story to the familiar rise of a Horatio Alger hero. But none of Alger's Plucky Dicks ever started from so humble a station, and certainly none of them ever reached such heights. Alger, a man of little imagination, thought his heroes had attained the pinnacle of worldly success if they became president of a bank. But Patiño can buy and sell banks as though they were bananas. He has accumulated a fortune of four billion dollars, villas in Biarritz, three big million-dollar palaces in Cochabamba, and a Paris mansion done with the gilded opulence of a Moorish harem, complete with Renaissance ceilings, damask-hung walls, and eight million dollars' worth of Rembrandts, El Grecos, good and bad Corots, Watteaus and Titians.

The man born in a hut not only possessed ultimately this "main house" at 32 Avenue Foch, but he could also live, when he chose, in his secondary residence, Château de Valrose in Nice, or in one of his villas or castles. He acquired railroads and banks; steamship lines and munitions companies; oil wells, mines and smelters; liquor monopolies, linoleum concerns, tramway systems; electric, waterpower and lighting plants; vast farms and vineyards; and a chestful of medals.

Few men in the history of the world could have done what Patiño did when the Chaco War between Bolivia and Paraguay ended his many interests contributing taxes to the Bolivian treasury to the tune of $194,000,000 to pay for his country's three years of conflict, the bloodiest in South American history.

This man whose immediate ancestry is the subject of doubt and joking speculation by his enemies lived to see his son marry the Bourbon Princess Cristina, one pretty daughter wedded to the Marquis del Merito and another the wife of a brilliant fellow countryman. Patiño had a third sultry daughter. He offered a dowry of forty million gold francs to go with this beauty, who became the bride of the doubly fortunate Count de Boisrouvray, of the French nobility.

Of course it is only Patiño's enemies who make nasty remarks about his birth—the gossipy *cholos* and Quechua

Indians who hate him for the starvation wages he pays, and the proud whites who regard him contemptuously for his *mestizo* blood and envy him for his unparalleled wealth. These people whisper that he is the product of a match between a wanderer and an Indian scrub girl who begot him conveniently in an unusual arbor of Bolivian love only two kilometers from the plaza.

In his native Cochabamba, it's sure, the Patiños are known as good and respectable people who had been married in the Roman Catholic Church, which they attended faithfully. In their veins ran the blood of pure Indian natives, mixed with the hot fluid of Spanish Conquistadores who had taken their will of Andean women, by wooing or by force as the occasion demanded. A distinguished Spanish explorer was known to be a Patiño ancestor.

Probably the first *cholo* Patiño was the love child of a Quechua girl and one of the white invaders. The Quechua lived in the high cordilleras of upper Peru, where Pizarro in his search for El Dorado found them subjugated and enslaved by the conquering Incas.

The persistent legend of Simon Patiño's unusual birth has a natural source, and the story is related not too disrespectfully. For a Spanish proverb foretells great riches for the son of a union thus consummated. When the ignorant workers, who believe what they see, observed that Patiño had accumulated a billion dollars, a sum utterly beyond their comprehension, and when they saw that his millionaire son, Antenor, had won the $100,000 Buenos

Aires lottery, they were convinced of his legendary conception. Such fortune could originate in no other way.

Nor is it entirely a disgrace to be of legendary or disputed birth in Bolivia. Such occurrences are common in a land so unorthodox. Many native women consider it the highest reward of motherhood to bear a child whose birth becomes legend, or at least one of which stories are passed on from generation to generation. It is an honor which brings with it an amazing respect and envy. Such mothers point with pride to offspring so fortunately conceived.

"There are Carmen and Juan and Guillermo," they will say. "These are children of simple birth. But ah, see Maria! She has a story!"

And without further provocation, the story will be told at length and with elaboration. Of such a custom were the disputed legends of Patiño's birth conceived, and thenceforth blossomed into oft-repeated fable.

It was into such a simple, unlettered pattern of living that Simon Patiño was born. A child such as he could look forward only to a hopeless routine of hard toil through endless days, of lowly work and ignorance. His parents and all of his forebears had lived by a code of servility, which is the immemorial destiny of the nationals of mixed blood in this paradoxical nation. They were men and women who lived without inspiration, without imagination. Only a pitiful few of their class had ever climbed to a higher level. Simon Patiño's father was considered fortunate that fate had given him talents which enabled him to become a shoemaker instead of a field or mine worker.

As it turned out, the elder Patiño's greatest luck was the birth of his tiny son, who brought him more fame and wealth than all the proverbially lucky children before him had ever succeeded in amassing in the history of Bolivia—more than all Bolivians put together, no matter what their condition of birth.

The circumstances of this fabulously lucky birth vary according to the mood, sentiments or birthplace of the man who is telling the story of that historic event. In Paris and Madrid, where Patiño is so magnificent a figure in the social and economic worlds, there are historians who assert solemnly that he was well born, never worked with his hands, and came of wealthy and aristocratic parents who gave their offspring every advantage that money could buy before and after his birth. They regard any other version as unthinkable.

In La Paz and the Argentine, there are many who say that the wanderer legend is the only true one. The story has recurred insistently, and there are also gossipy elaborators of legend who swear, confidentially, that Patiño is the great-grandson of the Argentine patriot, José de San Martín, or again that he stems directly from Bolivar, and yet again that he traces back to the traitorous Colombian general, Francisco de Paula Santander.

In the back country, some Quechuas and Aymaras hold Patiño in superstitious awe. They believe he is really the counterpart of the Inca's divine Viracocha, who was born miraculously of the white foam of waters as heaven's floods engulfed all the earth except the lofty Andean peaks which held the cloud land in safety. To them his wealth and power have become the incarnation of glory enjoyed only by Viracocha himself, who introduced the supreme being Pachacamac to the world.

But the truth of Patiño's birth, as far as anyone can determine, is perhaps the simple story perpetuated in his home town. There is evidence aplenty in Cochabamba that Patiño came into the world under conditions which would be considered shocking today, but in their time and place were most conventional.

It is, in brief, a story that is the only proper prelude to a life of contradictions, a life that has no parallel.

Patiño's obscure birth and his astounding good luck in making money, as for example his son's winning of the Buenos Aires lottery, gave rise to legend. . . . Stop However none of my pipe lines here will go on record that he was so born Stop All they will say his parents were modest obscure folk stop.— From a cable sent by an American correspondent.

2

The Prescription of a Witch

THIS STORY of Patiño's birthday begins at daybreak on a June morning in 1862. It is one of the most credible legends about Patiño, and it begins with a wizened old witch named Sofia, the best witch in the capital of the *departmento*. Sofia was a member of the Chiriguanos tribe, most primitive in Bolivia, and her magic powers were the envy of all the country's learned medicine men, even the accomplished Aymara and Quechua soothsayers. Her miracles were so numerous that even Sofia had come to believe that she could communicate with the gods and persuade them against their will.

On the June morning of Patiño's birth, Sofia watched anxiously until the sun, the great mountain-climbing "Bolivian stove," heaved itself abruptly over the crest of the cordilleras and threw itself on the roof of the world. The long, hard climb of this toiling red ball was a daily source of wonder and fear to Cochabamba's early-rising Indians. They were always relieved when the sun leveled off and left the threatening monsters of the mountains behind, because this was visible proof that the gods were awake and working. They shuddered to think of what would happen if the gods should ever sleep and not push the sun over that barrier of peaks 23,000 feet high. The sun, they believed, needed gods. Even gods needed gods to help them, not excepting the sun god, Pachacamac.

Thus Sofia was relieved to find that another day was indeed assured, that she would not have to use her wizardry to postpone the inevitable end of the world. It would be a particularly good day, this day, because it would begin with a job she relished above all others. Sofia pattered down the cobbled streets of Cochabamba in a great hurry, past the Plaza 14 de Septiembre, toward the town's slums where the Patiño family lived.

With her tongue she licked the taste buds in her mouth furiously, and bit on them with her gums to produce more saliva. She mixed the resulting sputum with green juices of narcotic coca leaves in such quantity that her copious mouth began to run over at the corners, and the syrupy liquid coursed downward along the wrinkled grooves of age.

Sofia had worked up this fine quid in order to earn an honest penny or two by spitting the contents of her mouth into the face of the Patiño baby; the midwife who had delivered it a few hours before had assured her it was one of the smallest infants ever born in Bolivia.

The witch's mouth was so full of the nauseous liquid that she could not talk to herself as usual, but she hummed nasally instead, in the general direction of the little Indian boy who trotted faithfully beside her. Sofia had ordered him to accompany her as a salesman, in case the new mother needed convincing. The ragged youngster stole admiring sidewise glances at her as he hustled along, running to keep up. As a reward, Sofia had promised to tell him some of her tribal secrets.

If Patiño were to suffer this primitive baptism, he could not have picked a better witch to officiate. Sofia had been chosen originally for her high office, by the sorcerers of her tribe, because of her lips. "Full lips," the tribal law ran, "are for kissing. Thin lips are for spitting."

Sofia was obviously well qualified. Even now, with her mouth filled prodigiously, pressing some of her deep cheek wrinkles almost smooth and forcing her face outward into a piglike snout, it was evident that her lips were like two sharp lines, no thicker than a widow spider's thread in a gunsight. Thus equipped, she could project her load with power and finesse. Cochabamba's infants were not the only objects of her accuracy, for many a startled adult citizen had been almost drowned after seeking the witch's brew as a cure for his afflictions. To cure stomach aches and teething pains, for instance, Sofia spat tobacco juice produced by chewing the pungent black weed of the wild Beni land. Coca juice, however, had powers exclusively its own and was to be directed at promising infants like Simon Patiño. His unusual smallness set him apart from other arrivals, and Sofia felt that her enchantments were challenged, that if she could succeed in making this baby grow properly, her substantial fame would be further increased and she could hope to add a few coppers to her hoard.

The Patiño family had risen long before Sofia started her journey, long before the usual rising hour of 4 A.M., when the lowly people of Cochabamba began their labor in the fields and pits for as little as five cents per day.

Señora Maria Patiño had roused shortly after midnight on that momentous June 1. Her groans awakened her restless husband, who sprang out of bed and ran to wake up the ancient midwife who lived near by in a miserable pile of adobe and straw. Eugenio Patiño was a desperately poor man. None of his children, of which the burgeoning Simon was the fourth, had been brought into the world by a doctor. The midwife would get a pair of his own hand-made sandals as her fee. The extra leather was ready in his cobbler shop; he had saved it for the purpose.

Eugenio brought the foul-smelling old woman back with him, and the hag lived up to her excellent reputation by pulling forth, a short time later, a howling boy child whose cries jarred in an off-key *obbligato* against the deep morning tones of Cochabamba's many cathedral bells, solemnly calling the devout to early mass.

Señora Patiño looked at her child lovingly.

"How little he is," she murmured.

The midwife looked him over carefully and nodded.

"Yes, he is the smallest born in Cochabamba this year," she declared.

"But he is sound?" the mother inquired anxiously.

"Aye," the crone reassured her. "He is sound. But so small! It is a pity."

"He will grow," Señora Patiño said confidently.

The midwife looked doubtful.

"Perhaps," she said, "but not to be a big man. However, there is a way to stretch him. I could call in old Sofia. She would make him grow."

This was a testimonial to Sofia's reputation for spitting undersized babies into men of normal height, and even above the normal in some cases. Few Aymaras and Quechuas ever grew taller than five feet six inches.

"Shall I call in Sofia?" the midwife asked.

Señora Patiño shook her head.

"No, my little baby will grow."

She guided the infant's tiny lips to her triangular brown breast, and forthwith named him for Bolivia's liberator, Simon Bolivar. The middle name she gave him, Iturri, was her mother's.

For a moment the midwife looked down at mother and child, superstitiously doubtful that nature could be trusted to take its course without supernatural aid. Her doubts triumphed. When the mother slept at last, she tiptoed out and hurried to Sofia.

That was how Sofia had come to be hurrying through the Cochabamba streets at an hour early for her ancient bones. Nearing the humble Patiño dwelling, the urchin trotting at her side, she was startled by a quick burst of gunfire in the direction of the army barracks near the Hill of San Sebastian. The volleys came instantly closer and bullets spattered around them. The streets, deserted a moment ago except for a few peons with their donkeys and llamas, now came alive with grim-faced men carrying bayoneted French rifles and brandishing vicious jungle blades. A few screamed battle cries and fired their weapons aimlessly in the air as they ran toward the center of the disturbance, in the city's business quarter. Armed men appeared miraculously from nowhere. Fierce-looking half-breeds sprang from behind the doors of adobe shacks, yelling vile, defiant epithets. They rushed headlong toward what now appeared to be a full-scale battle.

The peons prodded their mules desperately out of the range of stray bullets buzzing past their ears, and flattened themselves against the baked mud houses. The women shrieked, bolted their doors, and threw themselves and their children on the dirt floors.

Old Sofia choked in alarm as she swallowed some of her green quid. Grasping the child by his wrist, she sprinted to the Patiño home. She burst through the single arched, squat doorway into the rotund structure made of stone, mud and straw, its interior barred from the street by the typical adobe wall built before the entrance.

Her precipitous appearance was greeted first by the

squealing of a litter of guinea pigs, kept as pets until they were fat enough to qualify as the principal ingredient of *chupe* stews. The noise awoke the infant Simon, whose eyes were already stinging from the heavy smoke of llama dung burning in a rock cradle in the center of the room. He lay beside his mother on a high straw mattress heaped upon an adobe bedstead. The elder Patiño, weary from the night, dozed fitfully on a woolly hide, near the rounded corner of the domed room where his crude work bench was piled with smelly, uncured leather. Three small boys, the remainder of the family, sprawled in another section of the open room on rag cushions covered with llama wool blankets.

All this dozing, weary household was startled into terrified wakefulness by Sofia's noisy appearance, the squealing of the guinea pigs and the yells of the baby. The boys in the corner joined in the discordant chorus, and the father hurried to his wife's bedside as though to protect her from the confusion. The mother prayed aloud.

At the height of the bedlam, the shooting outside stopped abruptly. It was succeeded by an almost tangible quiet that rolled through the streets and caused terrified citizens to swallow their sobs and cries. Only the infant Patiño's protesting voice echoed in the stillness, possibly a protest against having been born into a world which had immediately splashed his rude house with the blood of revolution and brought him a witch who wanted to spit in his face.

But Sofia's mission was in vain. In spite of her dark

warnings, and the eloquent pleas of her little salesman, the mother refused the sorceress' offices and Sofia had to waste the contents of her mouth upon the indignant backs of the guinea pigs, who retreated to their burrows in the dirt floor.

Sofia departed in disgust, but she lived long enough afterward to say, "I told you so." Patiño was a stunted youth and he grew to be only five feet four inches high. Wealth has equipped him with high-heeled shoes and $300 suits designed cunningly by Poole's of London to make him look taller, but when he stands naked in his green crystal shower bath today, the natural shrinkage of age brings him down to a scant five feet three inches.

Patiño has built himself a million-dollar tomb of gaudy blue marble, near one of his fabulous palaces in Cochabamba. When he is laid to rest there, however, he will need only the smallest of coffins.

"So far as England is concerned, Bolivia no longer exists."—Queen Victoria.

3

Peaks of Terror

THE WORLD into which the little Simon Patiño came was a fantastic one, judged by standards of the world outside the towering isolation of the Bolivian plateau. The drama of Patiño's birth was typical of the national character—a mixture of pagan superstition, Catholic faith and the harsh sectarian dogma of extreme poverty.

Sofia and her kind practiced their magic openly outside cathedrals, where mothers left their babies in boxes or carriages (depending on their social position) while they attended services and prayed for the health of their children. The parents took no chances. As orthodox Catholics, they murmured supplications in the cathedral for the recovery of their ailing babies, while outside the old crones and their spittle worked the magic of pagan gods directly upon the children.

Witches were secure in Bolivia because the high rate of infant mortality—700 out of every 1,000 died annually—made every expectant mother abnormally fearful and consequently a willing victim of fraudulent diviners. Disease, poor food, heredity and superstition all contributed to maintain this unhealthy state.

But the fears of Bolivian mothers also increased the power of the Church, sometimes far out of proportion to the population in some provinces. In one small *departmento* alone, Indian labor built fifteen handsome stone cathedrals and 210 chapels, in which more than 500 ceremonies were held annually. Bolivians were extremely faithful churchgoers, and their piousness inevitably led to the stifling of industrial and agricultural progress. When the church bells rang, the workers dropped their tools, got their bottles of *chicha mescada* (an alcoholic mixture of saliva and fermented chewed corn), and adorned themselves with chicken-feather dusters and the skins of bulls. Then they went to worship God in a state of drunkenness.

Christianity and paganism were inextricably tangled in the strange pattern of Bolivian religion. The fanatical communicants brought to their worship a fervent Inca cultism which the priests could not eliminate. Thus the orthodox observance of religious festivals would be followed by orgies of flagellation and immorality, idolatrous worship of the sun, and saturnalias of license. The result was a compromise, hodgepodge kind of Catholicism which had no counterpart anywhere in the world. Prayers went up from 1,500,000 Indian and half-breed souls simultaneously to the Christian God and to the ghosts of Manco-Capac and his wife and sister, Mama-Ocllo, chil-

Wide World Photos

Simon Iturri Patiño

Wide World Photos

Mrs. Christina Patiño, daughter-in-law of Patiño

Wide World Photos

Antenor Patiño, son of Patiño

Wide World Photos

Bird's-eye view of Bolivian tin mining plant

Fenno Jacobs, from Three Lions

Miners praying before a shrine at the bottom of the Llallagua tin mine

dren of the Sun who came mysteriously out of the mists of Lake Titicaca.

In the competition for souls between the witches and the priests, the priests came out far ahead in a material as well as a religious way. The Church in Bolivia was not the force for good that it was in some other parts of South America. It exploited the population mercilessly, taking tribute in flocks, grain and money. The clergy demanded exorbitant baptismal and death fees, and levied tributes of all kinds, including personal household service.

Long before Patiño had undertaken his grandiose plans, the Church devised its own plan for enrichment in the abominable *alferezado.* This was a system by which thousands of Indians were appointed every year to "attend" a saint during religious festivals. These worshipers were required to bring mountainous offerings of food and valuables to the priests as penance for their sins, and they complied faithfully, piling up abundant riches before the altars of chapels and cathedrals alike. The priests used what they needed for their own subsistence and sold what remained, at outrageous prices, back to the same Indians who had made the holy sacrifice at such cost to their pitiful fortunes.

At the same time, the bedeviled inhabitants of the cloud land were also under the spell of the sorcerers. They contributed their most beautiful daughters to the debauchery of these diviners, so that the self-appointed "Sons of God" would not be lonesome on their nocturnal pilgrimages to Heaven, where they would intercede for the health and prosperity of Bolivian villages. Further, these celestial excursions required the spokesman to carry offerings of gold and silver, as well as food and clothing.

The medicine men operated at a lower level than the *shamans,* the sorcerers, but they were no less effective. They sold cures for all diseases, at whatever the traffic would bear. Some cures were secret herbs. Others were careful blends of known charms, such as ground peccary teeth, parrot oil, chips of armadillo flesh, the notched tongues of toucans, the urine of a pregnant mother, a bit of goat's bladder, or the gall of a red spider monkey. When one of the medicine men attended an expectant mother, he spun the woman dizzily so that the baby would not settle and stick to the womb; if the child was born deformed, it was quite obvious that it had stuck.

Other medicine men, the most primitive of the clan, came from the untamed tribes in the savage Chaco Boreal. They journeyed everywhere in Bolivia, employing the most drastic remedies. In Sofia's own village, for example, they used the ancient sucking treatment for every conceivable ache or pain. Applying their mouths to head, limb or torso, they drew in with lip and tongue the offender responsible for the trouble, and the offenders took many demonstrable forms—tiny green snakes, the ear of a dog, a rusty spike, a toenail, balls of wet cat hair. These men cured suspected insanity in children by placing the suffering youngsters for hours under the stabbing rays of the sun so that their bodies would become too hot for the devils to linger there. If the children died, they were considered better off anyway, because the devils had proved themselves resistant to heat and obviously would have occupied their chosen mortal forever.

All this was Bolivia at the time of Patiño's birth. The inhabitants of the queer, sad land were matched in strangeness by the hairy, shell-backed and feathered fauna. There were the armadillos, shuffling along like miniature, cadaver-eating prehistoric mammals. The llamas, crochety dyspeptics, spat and ruminated in their irritable way. And always over Cochabamba the high, thin air buoyed up the bareheaded condor, neck-ruffed and mite-ridden, circling lazily and patiently over impending death.

II

Politically and historically, Bolivia was likewise a strange land. To Quechua and Aymara alike, the most ancient traditions were subjugation and slaughter, endured through centuries of slavery and oppression under vicious overlords. Slaughter in the name of God, country, greed and lust had been approved by holy men, political leaders, Conquistadores, Inca chiefs and slave holders. Slaughter in the name of God had been sanctioned officially by Father Vicente de Valverde, spiritual adviser to Pizarro, the uncouth ex-swineherd of Estramadura, who despoiled the civilization of the ancient Incas over a territory 300 miles wide and more than

3,000 miles long, comprising nearly the whole of present-day Bolivia, Argentina, Colombia, Ecuador, Peru and Chile.

Pizarro's conquests put an end to the only era of comparative peace and security that Bolivia ever knew. It was an era that began, in legend, even before the coming of the Incas, when the great god Viracocha was born out of the raging flood of destruction which poured from heaven and inundated all the earth except the upland. The great Andean peaks held the top of the earth safe from the torrents, and on this dry spot, out of a chaos of wind and water, stepped the divine herald of the Supreme Being. Misty and luminous in his glory, exuding wisdom and breathing reverence for the creator of the universe, Viracocha brought to the world's surviving men a story of hope. He told of a Being beyond the imagination of man, whose grandeur was indescribable. Only through the Sun and the Moon, which this Being had created, could man even begin to realize the infinite glory of the true One. As a means of worship, Viracocha ordained that the Being should be idolized through the celestial bodies he had made.

The Supreme Being was given the name of the Sun, or Pachacamac, the giver of life, the custodian of souls, the teacher of behavior. As Pachacamac's representative on earth, Viracocha brought about a system of human relations so close to Utopian ideals of kindness and brotherly love that it impressed even the cutthroat Christians under Pizarro.

These ideals guided the Incas, who came after Viracocha. The civilization they built included care of the sick and aged, the first known "hospitalization" plan in history; and it boasted the first examples of old-age pension and social security laws. It was, in fact, a kind of true communism. No citizen could bequeath his property to any heir except the One who gave both life and death, Pachacamac. The Being gave wealth, and in his own good time he took it away by ending its owner's life. But at the same time, the principles of democracy were fiercely cherished through the belief that Pachacamac considered all men equal.

The first great Inca, Manco Capac, laid the foundations for his people's empire in the year 1054, and in spite of the ideals held by his nation, he did the job by the age-old methods of brutal conquest. Butchery and propaganda brought many tribes into the Inca fold. Manco Capac conquered the populous Quechua and Aymara tribes; he built paved roads, temples, aqueducts, thirty great and golden cities, and colossal fortresses, and he brought an unexampled prosperity to the land. He made Cuzco the capital of the Empire of the Sun. Befitting the ruler of such a powerful state, he robed himself in the trappings of majesty. His workers wove the royal fleece of the alpaca to provide him with white and gray garments, which were worked with designs of silver and gold. Innumerable mines supplied his craftsmen with the precious metal to fashion crowns, to weave decorative threads in the scarlet scarfs around his throat, to adorn the sacred bells, flowers and robes.

When Manco Capac died in 1107, in the fifty-third year of his reign, his subjects were so numerous that their total number could not be expressed by Incan mathematics. He left to his people an abundance of worldly goods and spiritual wisdom. In the half-century of his reign they had learned the value of vegetables to supplement their former diet of meat; they had mastered the art of molding metal and shaping granite, and of tin and copper craftsmanship. Fine examples of Incan architecture glorified the nation's art from the Andean plateaus down to the sea.

After Manco Capac came many Inca rulers, who acquired their authority through divine law, from Sinchi Rosa to Atahualpa. These chiefs added to their dominions by wars and diplomacy, until the power of the empire reached new and ever more impressive peaks.

At the height of glory, however, came the beginnings of disaster. It was first intimated in the dream of an Incan ruler named Huayna-Capac, in 1483. In his vision the aging chieftain saw a remarkable ship descending from the heavens upon the Inca world, its crew composed of powerful strangers resembling Viracocha, come in great numbers to conquer the empire. On his deathbed, Huayna-Capac called to his side his son and heir, the weakling Huascar, and told him of the vision.

"Be courteous to these strangers," he commanded. "Show them hospitality. They will be the representatives of Pachacamac, and they will be entitled to respect."

Huascar gave his solemn promise to abide by his father's wishes. He kept his word, but in keeping it he precipitated the complete downfall and utter destruction of his people. First he warred against his bastard brother, Atahualpa, whose father had bequeathed him the northern part of the empire. Atahualpa was victorious and threw the feeble Huascar into prison, after which he assumed command of the nation. The prisoner devoted his solitary hours to prayer, muttering hourly petitions to the Sun god. His lamentations were loud enough for everyone to hear, and they lasted long enough for him to receive what he thought was actually a divine answer. Remembering his father's prophecy, he prayed that the strangers would come and thus deliver him from bondage.

One day Huascar learned that the prophecy had come to pass. The ship his father had visioned was already landed on Inca shores, and a whole boatload of Viracochas was en route to the palace of his hated brother.

Huascar believed his freedom was at hand. Overjoyed, he fell upon his knees, gave thanks to Pachacamac, and summoned a fleet runner, to whom he whispered careful instructions. The runner was to deliver to the strangers a bill of complaints from the imprisoned ex-ruler, itemizing the wrongs which had been done to a man of royal blood and beseeching help to restore him to rightful leadership. Huascar's servant ran speedily and intercepted the band of 150 men long before they arrived at the gates of the palace in Cajamarca. He poured out his long message to a man with mean and narrow eyes. It was the butcher Pizarro. The Spaniard understood the situation at once.

"This will be our cause," he exulted. "Vengeance for the wrongs of Huascar!"

It was his excuse to rob and despoil. Pizarro bellowed pious orders for a great "march of liberation." How the Spaniards survived that march is a historic mystery. Day after day they struggled across deserts, and swam rivers swollen by melting ice and snow. The blistering sun of the lowlands burned them by day; and at night, as they scaled the heights of the cordilleras, they shivered around campfires which held the bones and ashes of Indian dead whose tombs they violated for dry fuel. But at last they sighted the peaceful city of Cajamarca. Pizarro, standing before his emaciated followers, muttered only one word: "Oro!"

Gold! That was to be the reward for their privations, and the thought gave the adventurers new life. They begged for permission to charge the fortress city, but Pizarro restrained them. He had a better plan.

It was a historic strategy, perpetuated in the history books, by which Atahualpa was lured from his stronghold and away from the protection of his warriors. He left the palace entirely unattended, except for a few servants.

The Inca chief appeared in all the glory of a great ruler. Wearing golden robes, he rode in a palanquin of solid gold whose four arms were molded of the same metal. The sight of this treasure inflamed the Spaniards' greed, and even Pizarro was impatient to attack, but he was restrained by Father Alverde, who stepped toward the Inca. According to South American historians, the priest said:

"I, my son, have come from afar with a great and holy message. It is from the Pope, the Bishop of Rome, the Supreme Pontiff and head of the Roman Catholic Church, the Vicar of Christ and successor of St. Peter, independent sovereign prince and the world's mightiest Emperor. He it is who has sent me to tell you that here is Don Francisco Pizarro, who has come to reveal to you the true faith of our Lord Jesus Christ, who died for men. You are asked to pay Him homage and obey His laws."

Atahualpa listened gravely. He reflected for several moments before he answered: "You cannot say I am your son. Only Pachacamac may call me son. He is my god and neither I, nor my people, want to change him. In our glorious history the Incas have paid tribute and homage only to Pachacamac, never to a living man, and so it is with your powerful King. Who is he? It would be a bad bargain to change from our god Pachacamac, who lives, for your God, who died. You appear to have two Gods and we have but one. And what is your proof of your God's invincibility? Show me!"

The priest, astounded and taken aback by the Inca's sacrilege, offered him the Bible and Atahualpa took it. He held it close to his face. He smelled it and twisted it.

He pressed it close to his ear and listened attentively. Atahualpa frowned. There was no life in the white man's God.

"You call *this* power?" he demanded scornfully. "This is no proof!"

The Inca king tossed the holy Book irreverently to the ground, and smiled almost pityingly. The priest was outraged. He turned to Pizarro and shouted: "Sacrilege! He has desecrated the Bible!"

That was all Pizarro needed. At his signal, the invaders fired their arquebuses and charged the little Inca company with their lances. Pizarro himself stepped forward and cut down the defenseless Atahualpa.

It was only the beginning of the slaughter. The Spaniards, shouting for the glory of God, descended on the Inca city, left helpless by the departure of Atahualpa's army, which had fled because it believed that Viracocha himself was in command of the strangers. Before the sun went down, five thousand "pagans" lay dead. Not a single Spaniard was killed.

After this noble victory the gold-crazed adventurers swarmed over the cloud land and into its villages, raping, torturing and extorting. Only one able leader ever rose again to defend his people. Long after Pizarro, the last Inca, Tupac Amaru, succeeded in inflaming his subjects to the point of desperation. They swarmed over thousands of square miles, killed the Spanish oppressors wholesale, and came within an inch of pushing the white men back into the sea from which they had come.

Tupac Amaru laid siege to La Paz, ordered his generals to take it at all costs, and forced the defenders to eat their pet cats before he withdrew. He destroyed the mile-high city of Sorata by loosing the dammed-up waters from Mt. Illampu's snow-crested heights and drowning the 20,000 inhabitants of the cordillera citadel.

But it was a lost cause. The Inca's poorly armed hordes were crushed by a superior army, led by the best officers of the alarmed gentry, and his people slipped back into a life of slavery—the men toiling all day in deep mines, the women unwilling members of harems, the children born into peonage. Tupac knew that he had fought in vain as he went to his death.

The formal sentence of death upon the last Inca was a masterpiece of ornate Spanish prose, prescribing details of mental and physical torture. He was not to be executed immediately. First he was taken to the great plaza of Cuzco, where thousands of bloodthirsty people waited in holiday mood. Tupac's wife, his three sons and a brother-in-law were brought forward in chains. All of them, and the chieftain himself, had been betrayed into the hands of the enemy by the Inca's most trusted lieutenant, Zumnario de Castro.

Tupac Amaru was impatient as a Spanish lieutenant strapped him to a chair.

"Hurry," he begged. "Let it be done."

"Not yet," the officer said grimly. "You will be last."

Then the Inca realized for the first time that his family would be slain while he watched. The manner of their death was most horrible. His wife's arms and legs were chopped off, spears were plunged through her stomach, and finally machetes were stabbed into her eyes. Tupac Amaru tried to turn his head away, but the guards seized his chin and twisted it back into place. As a punishment for daring to look away, a guard pulled the Inca's tongue out of his head. Still he was not allowed to die until his sons and brother-in-law were shredded slowly with sharp jungle blades and finally disemboweled.

When all the chieftain's loved ones were dead, the Spaniards freed him from his chair, bound his arms and legs with long cords, placed a noose around his neck, and tied the five lengths of rope to five wild horses. Attendants lashed the horses and guided their lunges in five directions. Tupac Amaru's arms, legs and head were ripped from his torso and later gathered up to be mounted upon high poles in towns which he had attacked, or from which he had recruited followers.

The Spaniards later ordered his property confiscated and proclaimed that all of his surviving relatives were to be denounced as infamous. All documents proving his unbroken Inca line were burned ceremoniously. But the last Inca's zeal for justice had lighted a fire throughout the land. From that moment on, the Spaniards feared even a wisp of smoke. They had seen a roaring holocaust.

The fire smoldered and sometimes flared violently within Bolivia's "borders of blood." In 1809, when the nation was still known as Upper Peru, its patriots began the long series of insurrections which were destined eventually to throw off the Spanish yoke. Even independence, however, failed to bring any peace to the burdened, melancholy people. The queer-chested, sandaled workers of Bolivia's frightening altitudes saw with despair that their heritage of blood and slavery had not ended with freedom from the Spaniards. There came the *caudillos*—the dictators—and the greedy mine owners, who learned, as the Spaniards had learned, that it was a simple task to enslave an illiterate and superstitious population. The Indians, lacking leadership and determination, submitted for the most part. Now and again they arose in foolhardy, poorly organized revolts, but they paid with their lives in unspeakable torture.

This, then, was the tradition of violence and death which Simon Patiño inherited and which became so much a part of his strange life. The bloody flurry in the streets on the morning of his birth was caused by a *caudillo* named Mariano Melgarejo, a dictator who had hacked his way to power with a bloody machete. His name was whispered in awe and terror at the moment of Patiño's birth. Patiño heard it later many times from the lips of his parents; Melgarejo was the bogeyman for Bolivian children. Yet it was Melgarejo who helped to carve the jagged boundary lines of his nation, and who was destined to shape Patiño's destiny.

The dictator's reign of terror, when Patiño was born, had reached new heights of cruelty. His ferocity and strength were attested by the street scenes visible on the morning of Patiño's birthday. Bodies sprawled grotesquely, block after block. Insurrectionist leaders hung from flag poles and street lamps. They had been strung up with nooses of wire, fashioned out of piano and harp strings ripped from instruments his men had looted from the homes of aristocratic leaders. The cruel steel cut throats like knives, and blood soon choked the gutters.

By a savage paradox, the funerals of these victims were occasions for rejoicing. The people believed that their dead ones were in heaven because they had opposed the dictator, and after services were over, the families hurried home to dance and drink the whole night through. Funeral processions were marred by drunken pallbearers and friends of the deceased; and sometimes the mourners, taking nips along the way, never arrived at the burial grounds. The processions of rich men, whose relatives could afford more liquor, sometimes reached the crypts only after half a dozen false starts, taking as many days.

But it was only the half-breeds of Cochabamba who behaved in this fashion. The few pure-blooded Indians who had survived centuries of mixed breeding, oppression and slaughter grieved for their dead in the most melancholy manner. For hours they sat in semicircles around the corpses, according to ancient custom, displaying a dignity and spiritual stature sharply opposed to their mixed-blooded neighbors.

It was the only conventional virtue remaining to them

from the Inca world, for by this time they had been driven into apathy. Most of them were drunken cocaine addicts, filthy human wreckage. To them, Melgarejo was only one more in a long line of ruthless oppressors stretching back through the bloody centuries.

Melgarejo was enough for the moment; but if the Indians had known it on that morning of June 1, 1862, still another threat to their future well-being lay squalling in the mean shop of a cobbler named Patiño.

The infant who was fated to carry on the Bolivian tradition of concentrated power was an intellectual product, at least, of the political philosophy which had made his country known as "the land of *caudillos*," the land of men who hacked their way to power with bloody machetes.

Simon Bolivar, the liberator, had no more than defined the boundaries of the country to which he gave his name before the unhappy land had to endure two decades of the *caudillo* Santa Cruz, who overthrew the duly elected General Sucre only a few hours after he took office under Bolivar's constitution. Thus the new nation began its history in an atmosphere of treachery, violence and deceit.

All the work of Bolivar, who wished his young republic to be a model of national honor and progress, was wasted. Bolivian heroes, who gave their lives in bloody fighting against armies of royalists, died in vain. Santa Cruz kept the land in turmoil. His cruelties and overwhelming ambition knew no bounds. He and most of those who followed him ruled by the sword. One chimerical constitution followed another.

The amazing procession of *caudillos* which followed Santa Cruz, after his overthrow by invading Argentinian armies and Bolivian revolutionists, provides a study in political instability which has few counterparts in world history. The very *caudillo* who finally drove Melgarejo across the high lake to Peru was responsible for crimes as heinous as any committed by his predecessor. This man, General Hilarion Grosele Daza, professed to have the interest of the country at heart, but his conduct in office was a record of looting, butchery and greed.

Corrupt and sex-mad, like Melgarejo himself, Daza owned a pearl-handled revolver of which he was inordinately proud. He was disappointed in it only because the smooth, hard surface of the pearl prevented him from notching the handle to represent the number of men he killed. Rather than part with his weapon, Daza used as a substitute a tree near his palace, which he notched every time he killed a man, woman or child, or won the favors of a virgin. Finally the trunk of the tall tree was scarred all the way to the lower limbs.

Daza's servile followers pointed to the tree and told him proudly: "You're a great man, master. The bark of the tree tells heroic tales. If only the whispering leaves could talk."

"They are eloquent enough," Daza replied, "but before I am dead, I will need an entire forest."

Fenno Jacobs, from Three Lions

Patiño mausoleum just outside Cochabamba

Kurt Severin, from Three Lions

Aymara Indian

Fenno Jacobs, from Three Lions

Quechua Indian mine worker

Keystone View Co.

As for Santa Cruz, he might have lasted in office until his death had he been satisfied to rule only Bolivia, but for years he looked acquisitively toward Peru and its untold treasures. At the height of his military power, in 1835, he invaded the neighboring country at the head of great forces, beat the defenders into submission and became dictator of both these mineral-rich lands at the same time.

Chile did not like this new arrangement, and Argentina's dictator, Rosas, liked it no better. Threatened from within and without his own country, Santa Cruz was finally toppled. One struggle followed another thereafter. Loot-hungry *caudillos* appeared on the scene, lasted for days, or months, and then were eliminated by stronger, jealous rivals who shot them in battle, poisoned them in jails, or cut their throats in quarrels. The nation was never given a chance to fulfill the destiny so ardently desired by Bolivar. Its people were kept in ignorance, encouraged in vices, educated in the art of murder, taught to respect brute force alone and appreciate most of all the virtues of espionage and deceit.

General Agustín Morales followed Daza. He was stabbed in the neck during a street fight and died from a severed jugular vein. A man named Ballivian seized power quickly and ruled for a year until he violated convention by dying a natural death. Then came Tomas Frias, who lasted two short years until Daza, who had meanwhile been collecting a new army, blasted his rival from the palace. Daza remained in the saddle for three years this time, until he was forced to get out for good at the beginning of the War of the Pacific, when Chile taught the dictator a few lessons in military strategy and wrested from Bolivia the port of Arica, its only outlet to the sea. This loss became the great national shame.

In the procession of dictators which followed that war there were Belzu, Córdoba, and Narcisco Campero—all leaders of armed camps. Some semblance of order and eight years of comparative peace followed Campero, who instituted during his dictatorship the tenth constitution Bolivians had been governed by since Bolivar wrote the first one. A few reforms were attempted by Campero's successor, Ismael Montes, especially in education and finance, but little progress was made in the short time he remained in office.

Four more years of peace came with the administration of Montes' successor, Gregorio Pacheco, in 1884, and a fairly calm period followed this when Anecito Arce took office in 1888. Arce was confronted with only one serious threat to his government, when General Camacho fostered a new rebellion and led strong forces against La Paz. Arce put down the revolt and served four full years.

A constitutional election in 1892 placed Mariano Baptista in power and he was almost constantly plagued by insurrections among the Indians and the sniping of Camacho, who continued to lead the country's revolutionary forces. Somehow Baptista survived his full term, but he was followed by Severo Fernandez Alonso, who held on to his seat in the Palace at La Paz with the greatest difficulty. Three years after he was sworn in, he was deposed by José Manuel Pando, who rounded up enough troops to win an easy revolution.

When Pando strutted into the Palace in 1899, Bolivia celebrated her seventy-fourth birthday. Those among the population who could count added up a total of sixty-four revolutions since the downfall of Sucre. Of the long list of presidents, six had met violent deaths, many had been exiled, and others had vanished under circumstances mysterious but by no means unusual.

Of them all, however, Mariano Melgarejo was probably the most spectacular. He typified all that was horrible in Bolivian political history. He was a fiend and proud of it. He was a murderer, and reveled in the knowledge. He was a debauchee, a drunkard, a liar, a thief. And he was also President of Bolivia.

Melgarejo's exploits are legendary now, but most of them are true. Bolivians still talk of his eccentric white charger, Holofernes. Before successful battles or guerrilla raids, the dictator provided his favorite mount with quarts of beer, and afterward he poured the animal a gallon of sparkling red wine.

The dictator was the darling of the half-breed masses, in spite of the fact that his armies had plundered from the fruitful Yungas valleys all the way to Sucre. He had raped many pretty young daughters of the white aristocrats to the north and south of Cochabamba. His aides were made happy with harems of picked beauties. Fabulous booty bulged his strong boxes and vaults in La Paz, and in a dozen secret hiding places scattered through his realm.

Melgarejo abrogated every liberty provided by the Constitution and assumed all public powers for himself. His rule over the lives of the people was complete. No citizen dared offend Holofernes, much less his master. Indeed, an idiot boy who had confusedly thrown a stone at the white charger while Melgarejo was riding to mass had been shot through the head by the great man.

Even more sacrosanct was the dictator's mistress, Juana Sanchez. He had enthroned her, nude and beautiful, upon a raised, velvet-draped platform in the Palace, surrounded by a thousand huge candles so that his generals might see her better. No fighting man qualified as an officer in the dictator's army unless he belonged to the pagan cult devoted to the worship of the *caudillo's* mistress, for Melgarejo had proclaimed his half-breed sweetheart a goddess only a few moments after he had blown off the top of President Belzu's head with a French pistol.

On many occasions, he personally undressed Juana before half of his Indian army, which marched single file past a bandstand upon which she stood revealed in all her nubile glory. Squads of picked soldiers with rifles were instructed to shoot down the first man who dared by word or expression to show the slightest disrespect.

On Melgarejo's birthday, his generals were treated to a closer view of the divine *cholo.* While Holofernes drank his vintage wine near by, not only the generals but scores of specially invited diplomats and representatives of many foreign countries feasted their eyes upon the firm, bare flesh of the brazen young beauty. After the guests had paid homage first to Juana, second to the *caudillo,* and third to Holofernes, in that order, they were invited to participate in drinking, open exhibitionistic licentiousness, and riotous, degenerate days and nights which eventually displayed the dictator's obsession for murder.

The master of these revels was born in 1810, 1818, or 1825, he wasn't sure which, of a mercenary arrangement between a certain Pedro Valencia, a procurer, and Maria Melgarejo, but his father ignored his birth and spent the time of accouchement attending to his business in a cut-rate whorehouse. The boy took the name of his harlot mother, and smoldered with deep, long, bitter thoughts about society. As he grew up, his sulphur and molasses complexion was surmounted by hair that was curled in oily mats atop a tousled, yaklike head. He was squat and muscular, with an angular jaw. Writers of the time say his "color was pale, ash-color red, as if a bilious and violent condition were beginning to make itself known. He had a large mouth with lips inclined to contract. His nose was short and easily dilated. His large eyes, dimmed and dispirited, were covered by soft, wrinkled upper eyelids. The small forehead seemed to flee from its base, to narrow further up, and to give to the back of his head an almost triangular shape. On seeing that small and sharply pointed head, one would say it wasn't made for thought. The face was edged with a dark, slightly gray beard which descended abundantly over his chest, giving a more masculine and somber air to the entire physiognomy. . . ."

Melgarejo's power was great for a decade or more, but his fantastic rule as President lasted for only six years before he was overthrown by General Daza, who seized La Paz and Juana simultaneously while the *caudillo* was away subjugating the Indians of Lake Titicaca's shores. Daza held Juana and her sister as hostages, threatening to slay them if Melgarejo tried to take La Paz. The deposed dictator made a half-hearted effort to rout Daza's troops, but loyalty to his mistress made him withdraw at the door of victory. He fled with a few followers. Holofernes was killed in the retreat. Melgarejo found sanctuary in Peru.

Rejected by all his supporters, even by Juana, who came in exile to the Peruvian capital, the mad ex-dictator sank into a state of the most sodden drunkenness. In an alcoholic daze, he tried once more, desperately, to see his beloved. He knocked loudly on the door of her house and pleaded, with tears streaming down his face, "Juana, Juana. I love you."

They were the last words he ever spoke. Juana's brother, José Aurelio Sanchez, opened the door and shot him through the left eye with Melgarejo's own pearl-handled revolver, which he had left behind in his love nest when he went forth to raid the Indians.

He lies today beneath a marble stone in the cemetery of San Eloy, in Lima.

The tradition of violence which reached its climax in Melgarejo has persisted down to the present in Bolivia, and the last manifestation of it was no later than the incident of December, 1943, when elements alleged to be pro-Nazi ousted the government of the pure Indian President Penaranda. For many months the United States, Great Britain and eighteen Latin-American nations withheld recognition of the new military junta, but all of them finally gave in and sent representatives to La Paz.

The revolutionists, led by a bespectacled social worker, Victor Pan Estenssoro, engineered a pre-dawn *coup* against Penaranda, who was friendly to the United States, and precipitated a bloody machine-gun battle in the streets of the capital which cost many lives. Estenssoro made Guabberto Villaorel president, and promised co-operation with the country's allies. The mob later rushed the house of the president, tore off the roof, looted the place, removed the plumbing and paraded the streets with Penaranda's porcelain *Yanqui* bathtub held aloft in contempt as a sort of battle flag. They shouted: "Down with North Americans! Down with the Jews!"

Thus the history of *caudillos* to date. Some of these men and the whole of Bolivian political history explain much of Patiño's career and the reason for many of his deeds.

Young Simon Patiño was born into a political climate

which promised anything but enduring wealth and power to a Bolivian leader. Patiño, who never even became president, transcended that climate and created a power of his own which no *caudillo* could overthrow.

The stories of how Señor Simon I. Patiño built up one of the greatest mining fortunes of all times vary considerably in detail.—From Tin, *a bulletin of the Pan American Union.*

4

"Dollars 250"

THE YOUTH of Simon Patiño was indistinguishable from that of most Bolivian youngsters. It consisted mostly of an unremitting struggle against his family's poverty. Official accounts of his life speak of his education in "private schools," although Bolivia was nearly totally illiterate at the time and the only school in Cochabamba was a private one far too expensive for Patiño to have attended. Nonetheless, the boy got an education of sorts and it was the generating spark to his career. When his parish priests taught him the alphabet and the fundamentals of grammar, they inspired and implemented an avid curiosity to know.

Like the young Lincoln, Patiño borrowed books everywhere he could and read them eagerly, particularly those about the early mineral conquests of the Conquistadores. His imagination was fired by the romance of early searchers for gold. All about him he saw examples of success and great riches made possible by the wealth in the multi-colored hills which framed his village, and he planned some day to have a gold mine of his own. His remarkable memory enabled him to store away everything that he read.

Hot after the wealth of the mountains, burning to save enough money for a claim, the young man began at the bottom as a clerk for the silver-mining Compañía Huanchaca de Bolivia, at a salary of less than fifteen dollars a week. Even this lowly position was higher than that to which any other half-Indian youth could aspire, and Patiño was able to occupy it only because he had achieved the miraculous ability to read and write.

The first real turn of his luck came when he fell in love with petite, attractive Albina Rodriguez, the daughter of a poor but white aristocrat of Oruro, a small merchant who had begun his career as a peddler.

At first the gulf between them appeared unbridgeable. Patiño was a poor matrimonial prospect even for one of his own class, but for Albina, who was both white and of aristocratic stock, the poor little *mestizo* did not even exist socially. Albina's blood line ran straight and true from a certain Juan Romualdo de Ocampo, who had been an informer to the King of Spain in Upper Peru. Her father, Tomas Rodriguez, was descended from Conquistadores on both sides of his family, and he was related to the notable Jacinto and Juan de Dios Rodriguez, Bolivian patriots who conspired as early as 1781 to revolt against Royalist Spain.

In spite of all this, Albina became the first of her ancient family to cross the line and marry a half-breed.

She knew the rules of Bolivia's haughty white society, but she happened to love her lowly suitor. Perhaps she saw something in Patiño to which others were blind. Certainly she had the utmost faith in him from the start, and she was determined to help him to the best of her ability. She listened, fascinated, while he quoted from memory long passages out of old books about mining, and her first advice to him was: "You must apply these things to yourself. And you will!"

Patiño adored her. He realized the sacrifice she had made to marry him; he had high respect for her white ancestry; and he had a fierce appreciation of her faith in him. He was determined to justify that faith.

Albina began to help not only him but his family. As a result of her prodding and influence, the senior Patiño rose miraculously from his cobbler's shop to become a local politician, then *prefecto* of the department of Potosí, an office which Patiño's authorized biography compares with the importance of a "state governor in the United States."

When they had been married five years, Albina went to work on her husband's career. She urged him to leave the mining company, and to accept a job that had been offered him in the prosperous wholesale and retail hardware store which advertised itself in huge red letters as "German Frick y Cía."

"Take this job," Albina told her husband. "It will enable you to get around more. Your chances will be better there."

The day he began work as underpaid clerk for German Frick y Cía. was the second luckiest day of Patiño's life. At the time, however, he thought it was the worst, because he came immediately under the thumb of the store's general manager, Ullo Krig, a sturdy Hamburgian whose watery blue eyes were framed by incongruous black lashes and bushy, startled eyebrows, topped by riotous baby-blond hair.

Krig's manner always indicated great concern for the welfare of a customer, particularly a cash customer. His approach flattered his humble clientele, and suggested an almost pious interest. Wealthy patrons called him "good old Krig." Poor Indians addressed him as padre, or as *tata,* which means "papa" in Quechua dialect. When he was accommodating a cash buyer, Krig's face lighted up with inspired benignity; his manner became more soothing than ever and his expression was as angelic and soulful as the sad eyes of a llama. Shoppers who found Krig in his best form rarely departed without merchandise, and when they had been sold down to their last coppers, Krig brought out a few imported British gumdrops to snare the last remaining coins.

Scarcely less unctious was the treatment Krig accorded customers whose credit records made them approved risks, but these he carefully refrained from overselling and did not, as a rule, turn upon them the full warmth of his personality. The fortunate few who were able to charge their purchases and still bask in Krig's favor were miners who had struck it rich in the hills, whose ore was already above ground, waiting only for a llama train to bring it down from the Andean heights.

German Frick y Cía.'s chief aim was to promote business with the miners whose claims were scattered over the Department. Krig considered only gold and silver miners as good risks; he had no respect, patience nor credit for those who were interested in such worthless metals as tin, tungsten, zinc or bismuth. Like the other gold and silver men, he had only contempt for the simple-minded Indians who had picked 100 long tons of tin out of a mountainside in 1861. No one knew what they had done with the useless stuff. No one cared, even when a doubtful tin market developed in Bolivia and a handful of miners worked a few small veins sporadically. Until 1894, Bolivia had produced a total of only 14,000 long tons of tin; a million tons had been thrown away in the mining of silver.

Krig was contemptuous of tin miners, but he saved the worst side of his character for delinquent debtors. This mood was always a shocking revelation to hitherto admiring customers. They watched him unbelievingly as he hissed their doom through gritting teeth, emitting unintelligible sounds and contorting his face.

In part, Krig was the victim of a system employed at that time by all South American merchandising firms, who gave unusual "responsibilities" to their general managers. These men were liable for credit extended to all customers. If one or all failed to pay, the firm held the manager good for the debt. A bonus system was paid on gross collections over and above a stipulated amount, representing the difference between the virtual poverty of a low fixed salary and the good living from a bonus. But unless the manager met a quota of gross sales, cash and credit, he faced a miserable existence in the year ahead. If he trusted men who failed to pay, it wiped out his reward.

To meet this situation, Krig had passed on a part of his burden to his clerk. Each underling was arbitrarily and unfairly saddled with a measure of the manager's responsibility, although he did not benefit in the slightest by the bonus plan. Even though Krig himself might have approved the credit for a delinquent customer, the clerk who served him was given notice promptly that he must make good the losses.

Krig's method of selling was one that his clerks could admire, in an apprehensive way. When a customer asked to see a hammer, for instance, Krig produced it speedily.

"Here it is, here it is," he said. "What is this?"

The Indian regarded the object carefully.

"It is a hammer, señor," he answered.

"It *is* a hammer," Frick agreed. "Is it a good hammer?"

The prospect balanced it carefully, inspected it at close range, rubbed the handle critically.

"Well, it feels and looks like a good hammer," he admitted.

"There!" Krig exclaimed. "It feels and looks like a good hammer. It *is* a good hammer. You are a good man.

You need a good hammer. Now a good man has a good hammer."

It was a sale. Next Krig handed the Indian an ax.

"What is this?" he demanded.

"This is an ax," the Indian replied.

"Well!" Krig said. "So it is, so it is!" He spoke as though he had suddenly discovered the most important fact in the world. "It *is* an ax! And is it a good ax?"

Then he went solemnly through the whole performance again. By this time the Indian felt important. The rich white merchant had repeatedly called him a good man. The customer was both delighted and flattered.

Krig sometimes used this sales approach when he called one of his employees to account, but the victim was never in the same state of mind and the dialogue was thus ironic. One morning the manager summoned Patiño. The little half-breed, trembling and wishing he had Albina with him, came into the presence. His boss handed him a piece of paper.

"Now what is this?" Krig inquired soothingly.

Patiño stared at the paper, fascinated. He knew by heart every column of its figures, every line of writing on it, every added notation by bookkeeper and boss, but he examined it nevertheless because Krig expected it of him. He stared at the white sheet and tried to concentrate on it, but his mind was reeling with terror. Krig regarded him carefully.

"What is that?" he repeated.

"Señor," Patiño muttered, "this is the bill."

"Ach," Krig assented. "It is the bill. It *is* the bill. And how much is the bill?"

"Dollars 250, señor," Patiño answered.

"So it is," Krig said. "Dollars 250 it is. And is that a lot of money?"

"It *is* a lot of money," the shaking clerk admitted.

"So it is, and you are responsible for it. The Indian who bought the goods was your customer. You oversold him. Look again and see."

Patiño studied the paper nervously. It listed dynamite, steel rods, coca leaves, dried lamb strips, yucca meal—everything a miner would need for survival under adverse conditions on a plateau varying in altitude from twelve to fifteen thousand feet above sea level. Patiño shook his head in rueful agreement.

"It is true, señor," he said. "I did sell the customer too much, but what can I do?"

"What can you do? What can you do?" Krig repeated. "He asks what can he do! There is much you can do. What is the amount of your life savings?"

Here it was. Patiño had expected it.

"Dollars 250, señor," he said.

"Yes, dollars 250. And where is this money?"

"In your vaults for safekeeping."

"So it is. So it is."

Krig whispered these words ominously while he smiled upon his employee.

"Go into the hills and find this Indian and get the money," Krig commanded.

"Money?" Patiño asked incredulously. "In the hills he will have no money."

"But in the heights he may have silver ore. And I will send in a llama train to bring it out. And you," he added, "don't come back without good news."

Patiño stumbled out of his employer's office in a daze, but before he closed the door, he heard Krig's parting words: "I am safe either way."

That unnerved Patiño more than ever.

From an obscure cradle, Simon Patiño crept into the mountains. Out he came with millions of dollars. Now, complete with princess, pictures, and palaces, he rides through the Bois on his way to a blue marble tomb.—Fortune Magazine, *May, 1932.*

5

The "Cry" of Tin

An hour later Patiño jogged out of Cochabamba on a borrowed mule, headed toward the forbidding Uncia mountains. It was to be the most momentous trip of his life, but the little *cholo* was so bemused at the time that he even forgot to bid Albina good-bye.

His goal was a tiny speck of geography more than seventy-five miles away, on the eastern slope of a saddle of the Andes, deep in lofty, unmapped acres. On one of these acres he might find a brown, human mite with ore worth dollars 250. Patiño did not give the difficulty of his mission a thought. He climbed doggedly up into the high serrations of an uninhabited plateau, devoid of foliage, a sounding board for the strato-gales which groaned over this bitter world.

Patiño made camp a dozen times before he arrived in the territory of the Indian's claim. On the long march he ate the food of the heights: *chunos,* small, bitter potatoes, frozen and preserved in the Andean glaciers and snow-banks; *chalona,* tough, jerked lamb strips; and brittle parched corn. He ate frugally of the scant fare. The traveler passed no habitation, no human being in the desolation of the heights. The only living things he saw were condors and queer, whining snowbirds, and once or twice an armadillo in the lower altitudes. He rode his mule on level stretches, walked and held onto the animal's tail when they pushed their way into the wilderness of crags. The mule was not saddled. Over his back, hanging on either side, was a balanced sack of oats; the supply had to last the entire round trip. Patiño fed the mule carefully, measuring by hand. Infrequent patches of blackened *stipa ichu* grass, which somehow found roots and survived in cold gravel beds, provided poor grazing for the hungry animal.

Altitude troubled both man and beast as they passed the 15,000-foot level. Of the two, Patiño endured the height better at first. For water, the man melted snow in the palms of his hand and lapped it, while the mule, acting on instinct, pressed his warm nose against ice banks and licked the trickles.

It was slow, tough going over a nightmarish terrain. The trek was further aggravated by the insidious Andean air, which absorbed the blood's oxygen and drained its red corpuscles. The heart raced and vision was distorted, so that the crazy angles of the cordilleras looked like a massive non-objective painting.

The mule had been breathing heavily for hours, and at last began to behave badly. His breath came in painful jerks, and he shuddered as he breathed. Suddenly he collapsed, and a wave of panic swept Patiño. It was as though a lifeboat had sprung a bad leak in a stormy sea, and the lone passenger had only a coffee cup for bailing. Patiño knelt down beside the animal. The mule's eyes popped glassily, swelled almost to the size of tangerines, but he was still alive. Patiño drew his knife blade from its horn sheath, grasped the mule firmly by the nose, and slashed the right nostril upward, then did the same to the left so that the animal could get the air his normal nostrils would not admit.

Patiño had seen the Indians of Cochabamba slice the noses of their mules many times before, but the crude surgery was always accompanied by applications of spider webs to stanch the bleeding. Here in this desolate region, however, there were no spiders; there were not even any insects except lice. But temperature came to the rescue of Patiño and his mule. The slicing of the second nostril was scarcely completed before freezing had congealed the first. Patiño ran his forefingers into the nostrils and removed the icy blood, so there would be no obstruction. The mule now breathed evenly; Patiño left him alone and made camp for the night. He was a tired little man and very much afraid. He wrapped himself in a blanket of llama wool, snuggled close to the mule's belly for warmth, and slept. He lay there with one of the animal's forelegs adjusted over his neck, the other used as a pillow, and he shared his blanket with the half-conscious animal.

Patiño was awakened by the mule's nervous jerkings.

For a moment he had difficulty remembering where he was. The strange half-light of the early mountain dawn disclosed a terrifying waste of gaunt peaks. It was snowing lightly. At one moment the air was still and the big flakes fell lazily the short distance from the lowering clouds; in the next instant they were whipped to crazy agitation by fierce gusts of wind.

The traveler's senses returned slowly. He rubbed his eyes and looked around for piles of llama dung. He needed enough to start a fire to warm his body, and to heat water for tea. But first Patiño prodded his mule with one foot and watched anxiously for a reaction. The mule shuddered and slowly got to its feet. The operation had saved his life; he snorted frozen blood from his mouth and wounds and began licking a snowbank for water. Patiño was overjoyed. He gave the animal a handful of oats, tethered him with a vine rope tied to a boulder, and went in search of the dung.

He walked several kilometers before he found a quantity dry enough to burn. Scooping it up with his hands, he dropped it into an empty oat sack and trudged back to his camp. He lighted the dung carefully with an old-fashioned lucifer match, blew on it and shielded it with his hands until the flame caught. Then he filled a kettle with snow and put it over the fire. In this altitude, where water would boil only at a high temperature, melting was a slow process and Patiño did not wait. When he finally gulped several drafts, he felt better. His spirits improved. He sat down to figure things out and eat a few grains of parched corn to fortify him for the march ahead.

He was not far now from the Indian debtor's claim, as nearly as he could estimate. It was an encouraging thought, and Patiño mused to himself: "After all, the Indian *may* have a pile of silver ore. My dollars 250 may yet be saved."

In a burst of new energy, he sprang to his feet and prepared for the last lap of his journey. There was still some climbing to do. The Indian had told him that his few hectares were located near the top of Salvadora Mountain, part of the Cordillera Real. Surrounding that greatest of the earth's reliefs were some of the highest peaks of the continent, a few more than 21,000 feet above sea level. It was over this awesome terrain that Patiño now had to toil. Bolivia's great mineralized belt lies in the higher realms of the Real, which extends from the Argentine border to Lake Titicaca, and Patiño had to climb to a height of nearly 17,000 feet before he could reach the Indian's mine.

It was tortuous going. The ordeal soon provoked new symptoms of altitude sickness. Patiño was nauseated, his head roared, little blood vessels burst in his eyes and the bloody tears froze crimson lines against his cheeks. Then, without warning, the temperature began dropping, as it did in this land where storms were born in a hurry. Freezing gusts whipped around the mountainsides and down from the looming peaks. Arctic cold gripped the high land.

When the mule dropped its dung the sections became ice-coated and froze before they hit the ground. The gas sealed within the dung by quick freezing exploded later like delayed time-bombs. When the storm ended as suddenly as it began, the echoes of these blasts cracked like pistol shots in the thin air. The reports flushed coveys of ice birds, darting like gray bullets against the rusty background of the peaks.

The dung explosions reverberated from the sound-box of the pinnacles and reached the ears of another man. Patiño heard the shout of a human being, a "halloo" which came to him so unmistakably that he halted his mule and stopped short. Excitedly he cupped his hands against his mouth and yelled with all his might. The effort nearly strangled him, but he stubbornly repeated the call as soon as he was able. He gasped for breath, waited and strained his ears for a response.

Again came the halloo. Patiño tried to answer, but his efforts were now too feeble. However, his first shouts had guided the other man, and soon Patiño saw a squat, poncho-covered figure approaching him in the distance. He recognized his customer.

The Indian, a Quechua, came on at a jog. He was bowlegged and weaved in a Japanese fashion, as Quechuas do when they are walking or running.

"*Buenos días, tata!*" the Indian exclaimed. He was glad to see his old friend.

For the moment Patiño forgot his slightly superior station in life and embraced the man wildly. In response the Indian gave him a more enthusiastic welcome than Quechuas normally show, because he liked the clerk who had trusted him with credit, and for seven months he had not seen another human being. His life had been without even a mule's companionship. When he had come up to his claim, he drove before him three male llamas loaded with the goods purchased at Frick's Cochabamba emporium, but he had long since killed and eaten the woolly animals.

The Indian spoke to Patiño in the choppy Quechua dialect.

"*Tata*, do you bring food?"

"I bring a few *chalona* strips and parched corn," Patiño replied. He fished in the oat sack and gave the man a piece of the leathery meat and a few grains of corn. The Indian devoured this offering ravenously.

"You are out of food?" Patiño inquired. "You look thin and worn."

"I have yet meal," the miner told him. "I ate my llamas sparingly. The corn is gone and the beans. There is only a little meal. I have been working very hard. Fortune has blessed me. I have struck rich veins."

Patiño thought, "Thank God! My dollars 250 are safe."

"It is time for me to go," the Indian said. "It is my plan to walk out of this upper world tomorrow."

"Then you will have company. I will go with you. I have come only to collect the bill for my company."

The Indian frowned.

"I have no money, señor."

"But ore. Of that you must have plenty."

"Yes, of ore I do have plenty."

"Then," Patiño suggested, "I only have to look, then carry a sample back to Krig. He will send in a llama train to bring it out, enough to pay your account and also for more goods."

"Yes, that will be good," the Indian agreed. "That will be very good and I can also eat."

The Quechua led the clerk to his claim. Great gashes in the mountainside attested to the Indian's amazing energy and enterprise. Mountainous piles of ore were arranged at the entrance to a tunnel he had dug deep into a looming cliff with his crude instruments. Gashes in the surrounding area showed where he had prospected unremittingly.

Patiño stared at the ore in amazement.

"You are a rich man!" he exclaimed. "That is, if the ore is good."

"If the ore is good," the Indian repeated; "and it *is* good. Some of it is almost pure."

"Then you have one of the richest mines in Bolivia!"

"I do."

In his excitement Patiño left the mule untethered and ran to the tunnel entrance, while the Indian trotted beside him.

"Here," said the Quechua, "this is a pure stick of silver. You could take that back." He handed Patiño a long, thin bar, and the clerk grasped it with trembling hands. It was silvery metal which the miner had chipped out with meticulous care from its bed in rotting shale. Patiño rubbed it and a hungry light came into his eyes. At that moment he believed the Indian was a millionaire, and he thought exultantly: "My dollars 250 are safe. Albina will be proud of me. Now we can buy our claim and maybe we, too, will be rich. And Krig will see that my judgment is sound."

"I knew all the time I was not overselling you," he bragged to the Indian.

"No," the Indian admitted, "you did not sell me enough. I have almost starved to death."

Patiño became expansive.

"Now you will not only eat," he said, "you will feast. This bar of silver alone is worth enough to buy a dozen hot meals and much *chicha* to wash them down."

"Much *chicha* and coca. Now I will have *chicha* and coca."

"All you want, all you want."

Patiño balanced the metal in his hand as though he could estimate from its weight how many meals it would buy. Abruptly he frowned. Something about the ore was wrong.

"Wait," he exclaimed, "this metal is light for silver. The feel is strange. Very light!"

The Quechua caught the alarm in his voice and pushed closer.

"Light?" he inquired.

Patiño did not answer. He held the bar close to his

eyes and stared at it as though he had lost his mind. He bent it backward and forward. The bar was pliable, which was not unusual with silver, but what nearly took the little man's senses was the scream which the metal emitted. It was a high shriek that pierced his ears. With a pitiable sob, Patiño threw the bar to the ground.

The bar was not silver. Patiño had heard the unmistakable "cry of tin," caused by its strongly marked crystalline structure. When it is bent back and forth, the crystals grind together and the cry results. Patiño had heard the "worthless" stuff scream in Krig's store, where occasional tin buyers tested the metal, and the cry now blasted all his hopes. He trembled all over and sat on the cold ground with his head in his hands. Over and over he muttered: "Fool's tin, fool's tin!"

The Indian was more philosophical.

"*Tata,*" he said, "I have worked months for nothing. Before I started working here I had nothing. I have nothing now. What have I lost?"

"I have lost everything," Patiño lamented. "Before you bought the goods to work the mine I had dollars 250. Now I have nothing. I have lost everything."

"I will give you the mine, *tata.* It must be worth *something.*"

Patiño thought desperately.

"A tin claim is worth nothing," he said, "but I will take it. In tin, it is a rich claim. I will try to trade it with Krig for the money I have in his vault, or part of it. Maybe he will have pity on me."

A few moments later the strangest, most momentous transaction in the world's mining history took place. Patiño disconsolately scribbled out a deed in pencil, turning over the mine to German Frick y Cía. of Cochabamba, in lieu of the owner's debt of $250. The Quechua, unable to write, made his mark beside the name his mother had called him. It was pronounced as Patiño wrote it, "Apac." The Quechuas have no written language and Patiño had to guess the spelling.

Apac came down from the heights with Patiño. They shared their food, but it was not enough and they were emaciated and weak when they arrived in Cochabamba many days later. Patiño walked like an automaton. He was lightheaded from starvation and crazed with forebodings. When they reached the entrance of the merchandising firm, the Indian said good-bye and disappeared forever, having set in motion a chain of spectacular events which would change the course of history.

As for Patiño, he entered the Frick establishment in despair, to talk things over with Krig. He was trembling again, his face was sad, and in his opaque eyes, now hollow and tired, there was only tragedy.

Krig greeted him cheerfully.

"Did the Indian have ore?" he asked.

"Yes, he had mountains of it," Patiño replied.

"Well, then," Krig said, with a trace of his old, unctious manner, "your dollars 250 are safe."

"But the mine is a tin mine."

Krig's smile froze, and for a moment he was taken aback. Then he laughed raucously.

"So he found a tin mine, a tin mine he found," Krig roared. "So the Indian had ore, mountains of ore. *Mountains* of ore, ach!"

Patiño was miserable. He squirmed. He was in a hurry to get to the point.

"The Indian paid off his debt with a deed to the claim," he said. Patiño got it out in a rush of words. His whole life, he thought, depended on Krig's reaction. Krig did not make him wait for it.

"The deed. Deed? Deed? We don't want any deed to a tin mine. Anyway, the debt is paid. Your dollars 250 have paid it."

"Well, I thought that you might take the deed and give me back dollars 100," Patiño stammered. "I thought you could do that much."

"Not dollars one," Krig snapped. "You keep the mine. It is all yours. Give me the deed."

Patiño handed over the crumpled paper bearing the Indian's mark. Krig read it quickly, with further amusement. In Patiño's laborious handwriting, the paper described the location of a mine called "La Salvadora," estimated the claim at about ten acres, located seventy-five miles southeast of Oruro, on the eastern watershed of the eastern range of the Andes, the Cordillera Real.

"It's a good deed, as far as deeds go," Krig remarked. "It's a good deed, I say, and it's all yours." He scribbled something on the paper, and thus signed over to Patiño the rights to the greatest fortune in the world. He wrote down his name, as executive secretary of the company, and gave Patiño a receipt for his dollars 250.

"That's just to make it legal," he observed. "Now you, get going."

Patiño walked out of the store. He had to see Albina now, and he yearned for their reunion as much as he dreaded it. But when he walked into his rude home, Albina greeted him as though he had just arrived for lunch after a morning's work at the store, instead of having been absent more than a month. Before he could begin an explanation, she spoke:

"Simon, you are tired. Sit down now and have your supper."

Patiño threw his arms around his tiny wife and he cried, for the first and last time in his life. He did not weep as a man would weep, but as a broken-hearted child.

"Albina," he sobbed, "we are ruined."

"No one is ever completely ruined," she told him. "I went to the store and I know all about it. Did you have any luck?"

"None. I tell you we are ruined. The Indian had only a tin claim. That is all we have. What will we do?"

"If that is all we have," Albina answered, "we must take care of all we have. When you have rested, we will go together to the mine."

High up in the thin, cold air of the Bolivian Andes, shrewd mestizo *Simon I. Patiño built for himself and his family an empire of tin. It was founded on the peon labor of mountain Indians whose lowly wage offset the high cost of transporting Patiño's ores to world markets.*—Time, *December 28, 1942.*

6

Everything Is Made of Tin

WITH THE energy and determination so characteristic of her, Albina borrowed money in small amounts from relatives, bought supplies, mules, rifles and ammunition, and set aside wages for four Indian workers. In a gesture equally characteristic, she took what remained and bought a small book about the history of tin.

Together the Patiños set out for their claim. At night, when their little caravan made camp in the crags, Albina read the history book aloud to her husband by the fitful light of *yareta* cactus and llama dung fires. The more Patiño heard about tin, the more enthusiastic he became. His imagination was fired by tin as it had once been stirred by the dream of gold.

Albina read: "The Egyptians used tin in 3700 B.C. to wrap their mummies. Tin is the most useful of the common metals. It made possible the thriving bronze industry of China, which got its start in 1800 B.C. Excavated ruins in Babylonia, Syria and Egypt have revealed bronze objects incredibly old, showing the curiously formed nodules were utilized by manufacturers of the most ancient times. Tin may have been the first metal used by man. The tin that Moses knew came from Cornwall. It is one of the six metals he names in the Book of Numbers, 1600 years before Christ was born. It made booty for the Midianites."

Some of these strange, big words were completely foreign to Patiño, but the priests had told him about Moses and he found it fascinating now to think that the Egyptians had used tin. Albina read to him whenever the cavalcade stopped on the march to eat. Before they reached the claim site, Patiño even learned about Homer, who wrote of tin in the *Iliad*. Albina explained a passage from it which particularly delighted the little man. The passage read:

"Next he placed around his breast a corselet which Cinyras once gave him to be a pledge of hospitality. For a great rumor was heard at Cyprus that the Greeks were about to sail to Troy in ships, wherefore he gave him this, gratifying the King. Ten bars, indeed [of the corselet] were of dark cyanus, twelve of gold and twenty of tin, and three serpents of Cyanus stretched toward the necks of each side like unto rainbows."

Albina told her husband that the curious breastplate made of gold and lead which Cinyras, King of Cyprus, presented to Agamemnon on his departure for the Trojan War also contained tin.

"It is all very romantic," Albina sighed.

"But tin is just scum in Bolivia," Patiño commented.

"It may not always be so," Albina remarked quietly. "We shall see."

One thing Albina's history book forgot to mention was that more tin existed currently than the world could use. The Patiños were in total ignorance of the world market for the metal, which was then used largely in the manufacture of key leads for pianos, pewter, ornaments, armaments, kitchenware, candlestick holders, candle-flame snuffers, toys, drain pipes, tea packing, Christmas tree decorations, bonbon wrappings and church bells.

Most of the world's supply at that time came from the terraced bowels of Britain's Cornwall mines at Eastpool, and the Great Dolcoath, where Caesar journeyed in search of the metal in 440 B.C., according to Herodotus. Caesar called England the Cassiterides, a name which has been applied to tin itself ever since. Cornwall, with its great tonnage, provided alloy which locksmiths used in making chastity belts for the wives of the Crusaders.

Bolivia had little apparent chance of competing with the easily accessible ore out of the Great Dolcoath. It was a remote country without smelters and manufacturing, a country without railroads and seaports, hemmed in by the Andes and by warring neighbors.

England, on the other hand, had already been profoundly affected by its tin supply, which had brought the Phoenician trader and the Roman occupation. Its Cornish ingots were carried to every part of the world. By the time Patiño was born, the Cornwall mines had produced 2,500,000 tons of tin since 500 B.C.; and while he was a clerk at Frick's, it was still turning out 10,000 tons annually, or 30 per cent of the world total. New deposits had been discovered in Germany, Czechoslovakia, Mexico, Austria, Spain, Portugal, China, Japan, the Federated and Unfederated Malay States and Indo-China.

The statistics, added up, presented a picture of world competition that would have discouraged even the redoubtable Albina. In the year the Patiños acquired their claim, tin had been discovered in South Africa, and Australian production had spurted to a point where it threatened to glut the world market.

In short, even if Bolivia had been able to reverse its position and could offer accessibility, the best transportation facilities and the finest smelters and foundries, Bolivian tin would still have been almost worthless on the day that the Patiños labored toward the summit of the Uncias.

But Simon and Albina were hopeful in their ignorance, and before long they had reached their claim and were embarked on their mining venture. They built a squat adobe hut and started housekeeping on the heights with a few kitchen pans and little else.

Patiño put the Indians to work with crude instruments, grubbing the sides of the tunnel their predecessor had driven into the mountain. The new owner worked as hard as his most energetic employee. He stopped only when attacks of altitude nausea forced him to lie down in his frozen shack under blankets of llama wool. For some reason, Albina was less susceptible to the sickness; she worked with her hands and supervised the Quechuas until Patiño recovered.

The Indians drove themselves constantly, in spite of the altitude, drugging themselves with the numbing cocaine of coca leaves. At first they worked past their normal endurance. Day after day in the tunnel they gashed for new veins of tin with their primitive tools. Two of them worked to open a new exploratory shaft, and their stone hammers and steel shovels sent rattling echoes through the high deserts of the heights. They began working before dawn and stopped only after darkness fell.

Albina cooked the scant meals for her husband and the workmen, but the Patiños consumed more food than their four laborers combined. The Indians' stomachs were coated with the green, narcotic coca juices, which spared the user such physical cravings as hunger and at the same time endowed him with superhuman energy and endurance.

For several weeks the Quechuas scarred the earth in search of a new, elusive vein of tin where the former worker had left off. They dragged tons of red dirt and rock to the opening, pushed it back with hoes, and finally, when the distance became too great, carried it out in sacks slung over their backs. But there was no evidence of the rich tin deposits the owners had anticipated. Patiño thought that enough dirt had been removed to prove the property. He was the first to give up hope.

"It's just our luck," he told Albina. "We have no tin here. Apac found a shallow vein and now it has run out."

"We will keep on," Albina said grimly. "I will not let you quit."

Patiño returned to his work with even more desperate energy. In those days he had not an ounce of excess fat, and he was capable of hard labor. He was little but strong; his thick neck rippled with muscles; his arms and legs were toughened and conditioned by years of grueling toil.

Temperamentally, however, Patiño was not a leader of men. He was sharp with his Indians, lashing out at them with undeserved rebukes. While the men were under the influence of coca, they endured this abuse almost cheerfully, because the Quechua never expects a kind word. But he will not work without his coca. This national curse, a major industry in Bolivia, produced eventually a nation of narcotic addicts, making thousands of men and women befogged pawns for the labor barons.

Six weeks passed on the top of Salvadora before Patiño had real trouble with his men. One morning, after he had aroused Albina, he strained his ears for the bedlam of noise which should be coming from the Indians at that hour of the morning, but there was only silence. Patiño wrapped himself in a poncho and hurried to investigate.

The Indians were awaiting his arrival, holding their woolen skull caps humbly in their hands.

"*Buenos días, tata,*" they said respectfully. "We must leave you."

"Leave?" Patiño asked incredulously. "Leave?"

"*Si, tata.* We must leave. We have no coca. We cannot work without coca." The Indians were nervous and strained. The muscles in their faces twitched, they licked their dry lips, and imaginary flies hummed near their ears.

Patiño raged at the men. He screamed so loudly that he tortured his lungs, but desperation made him forget the altitude. In the language of the Quechua, he called the Indians names and asked for the vengeance of their fierce thunder god, Chiroquello, to smite them. Alternately he berated and begged them, offering higher wages and more food.

"*Tata,*" the Indians said simply, "we want only coca." As he spoke, their leader tried to swat the imaginary fly.

Before Albina could dress herself, the Indians had gone. They trotted in single file down the mountainside in the direction of Cochabamba. Patiño never saw them again.

It was a lesson to the embryonic mine owner. He never again underestimated the Bolivian addict's craving for coca. When he became the great miner of Bolivia, he made certain that his workers always had ample supplies. His company stores sold it to all who toiled in the mines, at prices so low that even the poorest-paid Quechua could have enough of the drug to satisfy him. This policy was highly rewarding. Cocaine made his workers more amenable to discipline and gave them more energy to increase his riches.

But now Patiño and Albina were deserted in the dismal camp. They had only the company of their dour, gaunt llamas, who had been losing weight steadily on a diet of *stipa ichu* grass. Patiño was disconsolate.

"Now we *must* quit," he said. "Even our llamas will leave us. They will die soon of starvation."

"We will *not* leave," Albina told him once more. "We will try a little longer. We may uncover a vein and prove the mine."

"But if the llamas die, how can we carry the ore down to Cochabamba?" her husband protested.

Albina's eyes flashed. "We will carry it on our backs," she said firmly.

The grim routine of work went on. The Patiños arose even earlier than before, and by daybreak both were toiling deep in tunnel No. 1. They saw the sun only briefly when sacks of dirt and rock had to be lugged out to the exit, and when they stopped briefly for lunch.

It was a killing pace, maintained day after day. Patiño's labor was erratic and depended on his mood. Sometimes he grubbed the red dirt morosely, in a dull and dejected fashion. At other times he attacked the tunnel's sides like a madman until he retched. Albina could shake him out of his depressions only by quoting from her book on tin.

"Bronze cannot be made without tin," she repeated to him. "Pewter needs tin. Tin is a wonderful metal."

"But we have no tin," Patiño answered dazedly.

"We *will* have." Albina's voice held the same unwavering assurance.

His wife's optimism stimulated Patiño momentarily, but he was becoming more and more of a problem. Albina, knowing that he might give way momentarily, watched him anxiously in the dung-lit gloom of the tunnel and prayed for an early reward.

It was snowing lightly on the eighty-seventh evening of their camp on La Salvadora when the Patiños emerged from the tunnel and straightened their aching backs after eleven hours of steady toil. Their working day was done. A full moon, impaled on a neighboring peak, lighted the irregular landscape with an eerie glow.

The Patiños had dragged out a sack of rock from their furthest diggings, and they dumped it now on the growing refuse heap. White rocks and red dirt poured out of the worn receptacle. They were too weary to appreciate the little miracle by which the moon gold and the snow whiteness of the ore made a ghostly pattern, a pattern of wet crystal that spelled enchantment.

Albina was the first to notice that one of the big rocks which tumbled from the bag was different. In the moonlight she caught a reflected gleam of silver metal, holding tenuously to the granite. She grasped her husband's arm.

"Look, Simon," she whispered. "I think we have found it."

Patiño's dull eyes followed her pointing forefinger, and he fell upon his knees. He picked up the rock and examined it closely.

"*Estano!*" he exclaimed. "We have hit the vein."

Albina murmured the word almost in awe. "*Estano!*" She stood very still, but Patiño dug into the mound with his bare hands. Every piece of stone brought out in the last sack was rich with tin. With trembling, bleeding fingers he recovered one that was almost pure tin. He carried it over to his wife excitedly, and she held it in her hands and stared at it for a moment.

"Now we can go to Cochabamba," she said. "We have proved our mine." For the first time Albina seemed to notice the blue-white radiance of the moon on the snowy heights.

"Look," she said to Patiño, holding the pure ore before his eyes and waving her hand toward the vista about them. "It is just like that. *Semeja la luz de la luna en la nieve.* It looks like moonlight on snow!"

Next morning the Patiños did not rise until the sun had made a glittering prism of the glacier on a neighboring mountain. They could afford to be lazy now. Albina made scorching tea for their breakfast, and afterward Patiño entered the mine tunnel for a last look.

Fenno Jacobs, from Three Lions

Banco Mercantil, owned by Patiño, in La Paz

Acme Newspictures, Inc.

Fenno Jacobs, from Three Lions

Fenno Jacobs, from Three Lio

Indian girl in mining camp at Caracoles

When he came out he was smiling and in his face there was no vestige of the old depression.

"It is there!" he exclaimed. "It was no dream last night. There is a *wall* of tin ahead."

Patiño helped his wife fill a sack with samples of the ore.

"There is no need to break more," she said. "This is rich enough."

"Yes," Patiño assented, "it is high grade, fine. It will convince any man."

"We will need money now to break down the wall of tin," Albina said. "It is good that the ore is rich."

They struggled with the heavy sack of ore. It weighed eighty kilos, the maximum load a llama will carry. Making this burden fast upon the strongest animal, they secured their kitchen goods and blankets on another. During the long trip back to Cochabamba they alternated the loads to rest the llamas.

As they set out in high spirits, the frozen earth snapped beneath their feet like cracking carrots. The llamas stepped gingerly with their dainty feet, beating a sharp tattoo upon the ice. But the preoccupied travelers were not aware of these noises. They were absorbed in dreams of the things to come. It was Albina, however, who noticed the llamas' tinkling neck bells. The sounds were high and tinny.

"Those bells," Albina said, "hear them? They are tin. Tin is truly a useful metal."

Tough-muscled, lean, brown Indians on the high, cold plateau of the Andes, a Bolivian multimillionaire in Paris and a hard-working American business-man in a New York office. Laden llamas, like glorified goats, carrying heavy lit-tle sacks of tin ore down from the mountains to the railroad. British work-men in a smelting and refining plant across the Atlantic. And last of all, the American consumer, eating food out of a can made of tinplate, squeezing tooth paste and shaving cream out of tin tubes and listening on Sunday morn-ing to church bells that have 25 per cent tin in their composition.—From a story by Royal F. Munger, Chicago Daily News, *June 5, 1928.*

7

Tin Fever

PATIÑO COULD NOT have made his discovery at a more opportune time in the whole history of tin mining. It came at a moment when a revolution in tin had changed the face of the industry almost overnight.

The revolution had been developing unnoticed for a dozen years. Tin canning, hitherto regarded suspiciously, was on the threshold of its mushroom growth. In the year of Patiño's discovery, 1894, the age of steam and steel was making far greater demands than ever upon world resources—for bronze, for precision instruments, and for the strange horseless carriages which European manufacturers were beginning to produce.

No one, however, could have foreseen that in a few short decades the American people alone would be literally wallowing in tin, that the United States would be using 160,000,000,000 tin cans every year, or that tin-gobbling Detroit would use in one week the entire production of the Great Dolcoath.

In the month that Patiño and his wife drove their

llamas into Cochabamba, it was rumored in the city that the mines of Cornwall were running out. White strangers in European clothes had already arrived in the little town with the news that the fields of Bohemia and Germany's Saxony pits were nearly exhausted of the base metal. The strangers were there to "look around," they said.

At that moment the story of tin was at a breathless pause. Tin was still a relatively worthless metal in Bolivia, but the waning supply and the sharply increasing demand had made the "scum" of that country's mineral resources attractive for the first time to far-sighted tin speculators in other lands.

When the truth of the tin situation dawned suddenly on mining men everywhere, "tin fever" gripped the world overnight. Metallurgists raked the sands and broke the rocks of South Dakota's Black Hills in the search for traces of the metal. Others roamed the mountains of Virginia, North Carolina, South Carolina and other states. Only infinitesimal, commercially unimportant quantities were found.

Rough and ready financing went on everywhere. Prospectors discovered small quantities on a cold Alaskan coast near Cape Prince of Wales, and worked ice-cap mines with shivering, unwilling Eskimo laborers. The excitement following that strike surged out of control in the United States. Stock promoters issued brochures asserting that the finds of the Cape Mountain veins on the coast of the Bering Straits were "fabulous," worth perhaps $100,000,000.

The Nome *News* of September 25, 1903, published a breathless story about this find, which provides some indication of what Simon Patiño had stumbled upon far away on the Andean heights of Bolivia. The *News* proclaimed:

> One hundred million dollars' worth of tin will be taken out of one piece of ground three and one-half miles square on Cape Mountain at Cape Prince of Wales. This is not the dream of a Jules Verne or the mammoth fabrications of mining promoters, but arithmetical calculations made from ore in sight or within easy reach on the claims of the Bartels Tin Mining Company. . . . It means that the Bartels claims and those immediately adjoining will turn out more tin than Anvil, Glacier, Dexter, and all the creeks roundabout will ever turn out in gold. And the Bartels claims are only a small portion of those in the Arctic.
>
> W. J. C. Bartels, president of the company, is in Nome awaiting the arrival of the *Oregon*, on which he will start for New York. Speaking this morning in his modest way, for Mr. Bartels is a very modest man, he said:
>
> "It was the original purpose of the company to continue the work on Cape Prince of Wales claims all winter, but there was a breakage in an important piece of machinery of such a character that it had to be sent to the States for repairs. We are not in any way booming our company and there is little of its stock on the market. There are 5,000,000 shares which are now quoted at $5.25 a share, indicating a value of over $26,000,000—this, too, in spite of the fact that not a dollar's worth of Cape Prince of Wales tin has been sold commercially.
>
> "There is one dyke in our claims known as the Fourth of

July Group because discovered on Independence Day, which is from 1,600 to 1,800 feet thick and the lowest assay of cap tin is 2.40 per cent. The coming season the company will bring to Alaska five smelters of eight tons capacity each and this winter a full cargo of anthracite coal—for it takes anthracite to smelt tin—will be brought around the Horn from Philadelphia and stored until the opening of Behring Sea navigation at Dutch Harbor."

The claims of the Bartels Company are really a mountain of tin, with here and there copper ore in paying quantities. It is the purpose of the organization, when its machinery is all completed and at work, to turn out an average of 400 tons of refined tin every 24 hours. This, it is calculated, is just about what the United States consumes each day in the manufacture of tin goods. . . .

Preparations already under way will next season make this the biggest mining camp in Alaska. There is already on the ground 37 tons of provisions, 9,000 gallons of gasoline, and four miles of wire for electric ore trains. The freighter *Eureka* brings for the company seven and a half tons of dynamite. A gigantic windmill will be erected on the extreme western part of the property and the dynamos which will run all of the machinery will be run by it on windy days. . . .

Precisely just how much tin there is in this stupendous deposit of course no human being can know exactly, but it is quite safe to estimate that it will run $100,000,000, probably a great deal more. In round figures the stock of the company is now quoted at $26,250,000, and it is announced that its officers would not part with it for less than $40,000,000.

A later prospectus for the Bartels Company announced: "Stock is for sale now at the nominal price of ten cents per share. Shares are $1.00 each. We believe it worth *more than par intrinsically* and believe that natural and easy miner-like development during 1904 will place it above par on its actual showing of values. . . ."

Ten for one! Many Americans bought this stock and other Alaskan tin stock, but all the tin mined in the Arctic since its discovery would not supply the bearings for one year's output of Ford cars in Detroit. In the 53 years between the discovery of tin in North America in 1893 and the end of 1945, the whole continent did not produce two thousand tons. Today's workings in Alaska, South Dakota and California are no more than a drop in the world's supply.

The abortive Alaska boom was only an echo, nearly a decade later, of the long-range development which was taking place at the time Patiño came down from his mountain for the second time. The tin merchants of Europe were not interested in North America, then or ever. They knew about the quantities of "worthless" metal which the gold and silver miners of Bolivia had been throwing away for years, and the men they sent to "look around" were prospectors without pickaxes, vanguards of a tremendous new industry which would make the old tin industry look like idle digging.

The happy coincidence was another formidable example of Patiño luck. These farsighted emissaries from Europe, looking for tin resources, were scouting around Cochabamba at the moment Patiño came down from the mountain with the modest hope that he might be able to make a decent living out of his discovery.

Simon Patiño had the world's tin future wrapped up securely in a bag of ore and a scrawled-upon slip of paper.

A famous refugee from the caste system is the fabulous Patiño, who has piled one fortune on another, built a world-wide tin empire, served his country as an honorary diplomat, but lived in France and now the United States because his Indian blood has deprived him of social recognition in Bolivia.—Saturday Evening Post, *March 4, 1944.*

8

Don Simon!

News of the discovery on Salvadora's heights was not long in getting around. Coupled with the arrival of the strangers who were so willing to buy the hitherto worthless tin, it had a magical effect on all Bolivia. Silver miners who had thrown out tin ore now tried frantically to remember where they had found the richest pieces. Prospectors swarmed into the hills to stake claims in likely places, and there were many men in Cochabamba who were willing to lend money for new developments.

To one of these, an Englishman, Patiño made application for some cash. Albina went with her husband to negotiate the loan. She explained the riches of La Salvadora to the Britisher, showed him the *estano puro*, and described the wall of metal at the end of their tunnel. As a result of her sales talk, the Patiños walked out with a loan of $5,000 in the form of a draft on a Sucre bank, and in return the lender had a mortgage on La Salvadora.

Patiño and his wife left the office in high spirits.

Walking out into the bright Cochabamba sunlight, the little *mestizo* appeared transformed. He carried himself jauntily, shoulders erect and step buoyant, and in his eyes there was a new light which not even Albina had seen before. His long, straight lips, which once drooped indifferently, were now tight and firm, the left side curling in the faintest suggestion of a sneer. Patiño was a strutting little man on that first day of real victory. He was having his day in the sun and he loved it.

Fellow townsmen who had never before glanced his way now waved to him from opposite sides of the street. Some hailed him as "señor." The poor uncovered their heads at his approach. Venerable citizens greeted him warmly as "Simon."

"Do you hear, Albina?" he exclaimed. "They call me señor."

Patiño enjoyed his new role. He paraded the streets like a conquering hero. The air was rich and sweet; the skies were blue and warm. He stuck out his chest.

"Tin *does* have something!" he exulted.

"You are *el minero grande,*" Albina assured him.

"We are rich."

"Not now, but we will be, in time."

"Five thousand dollars is a lot of money. Let me see the draft."

Albina fished for it under her waist and handed the paper to her husband.

The story may be apocryphal, but older residents of Cochabamba swear that as Patiño studied the draft he got a sudden impulse to see Krig. They say that he snapped his fingers, stuffed the paper in his pockets, and grasped his wife by the wrist, saying: "Come with me, Albina." What followed may be only legend, but there are many oldtimers who agree on the story and assert without qualification that it is true.

At any rate, it is easy enough to believe that the arrival of the Patiños in the store of German Frick y Cía. caused a sensation. Customers and clerks alike gaped at the pair. Krig, busy with an Indian customer, saw the visitors last of all. He was serving a cash customer, who merited the full benefit of his technique, and he was thoroughly engrossed in the job of making a profit on the Indian's purchase. For several minutes he was unaware of the unnatural quiet in his emporium, while Patiño and his wife stood motionless a few yards away. Patiño studied his former employer with amusement. He knew every step of the technique by heart, but where it had once held him entranced, now it seemed only laughable. He wondered how he could ever have been afraid of this blond, comic man. Patiño reached into a pocket and pulled out the paper which was as valuable to him as the wealth of the Incas. Holding it aloft, he shouted: "Krig!"

The manager started, wheeled and faced his ex-clerk. Patiño's new fame had preceded him, and his exciting story was known to Krig, as it was to everyone in Cochabamba. Krig's rosy German cheeks turned the color of coffee beans, and he opened his mouth as though to speak, but no words came. He waved uncertainly the stick of dynamite he was holding, while the customers drew back anxiously. More timorous customers fled to the street. In the end, however, Krig could only make unintelligible noises; he was completely disorganized.

Patiño reached into another pocket and drew out a second paper. He pushed it under the German's nose.

"And what is this?" he demanded of the manager.

The sight of the paper covered Krig with still greater confusion, but somehow he managed a reply.

"Why, that is a paper," he said, "a receipt for your dollars 250."

"So it is, so it is," Patiño mimicked. "And why do I have this paper?"

"Why, why," Krig stuttered, "because of the mine."

"And so it is, so it is," Patiño tortured him. "And is the mine a good mine?"

"I hear it is a good mine," the unhappy man answered.

"Well," said Patiño, "it *is* a good mine. I am a good man. Now a good man has a good mine."

Krig bowed his head. It was enough, but Patiño would not let him go. He thrust the other paper under the manager's nose.

"And this, what is this?"

"Why, that, señor, is a draft."

"And how much is the draft?"

"It is dollars 5,000."

"So it is, so it is." Patiño was joyful now. "I have a

Press Association, Inc.

Bolivian troops in the Plaza Venezuela, La Paz

Fenno Jacobs, from Three Lions

Fenno Jacobs, from Three Lions

View of Colguiri, a Hochschild-owned tin mine 100 miles from La Paz

Fenno Jacobs, from Three Lions

mine and dollars 5,000. You have my dollars 250 and no mine. A good man has made a good swap."

With that Patiño stuffed the precious papers back into his pocket, and walked out of the store triumphantly with his wife. They say that Krig was never the same again.

After this victory, the Patiños rested for two weeks before they began to make plans for the exploitation of La Salvadora. They feasted on good food. Choice cuts of llama meat and delicacies from the best truck gardens of the *departmento* filled the cheap earthenware bowls on their table. All this helped in the transformation of Patiño. As he filled out physically, he also lost his manner of servility and became increasingly arrogant. Envious people began to say that Patiño was the only man in Cochabamba who could strut sitting down.

The Patiños also made some modest additions to their wardrobes. In Simon's case, the new clothes produced a somewhat startling effect. His new ill-fitting wool jacket, store shirt with removable celluloid collar and bright yellow tie emphasized his bilious bronze complexion and the startling proportions of his neck. Observers who looked past this contrast saw that Patiño had discarded his *ajotas,* the native, uncured leather sandals. He was wearing his first pair of shoes, a caste mark of major importance. They were uncomfortable, but Patiño knew that they were the symbols of his emancipation from the rest of suffering Bolivian humanity.

When Patiño laced his shoes for the first time, he became a changed man. He regarded his erstwhile state with scorn, and he had only contempt for those who had shared it with him. It was difficult for him to realize that he had ever been a member of the downtrodden multitude. He began to think of himself as one of the elect.

It *was* true that Patiño had already escaped the two worst fates which could befall a poor Bolivian. He was not a permanent member of the starving farm labor population, toiling in the orange, lemon and pomegranate acres of Bolivia's eastern section, where the world fell away from the mountains to altitudes of less than a thousand feet. Nor was he condemned to the life of the boil-ridden, drugged and underfed workers who suffered in the mines for five cents a day. But he knew what both fates were like, because he had been first with the coffee slaves, later with the lumbering peons in the *departmento's* rich forests, and still later with the drudges of the saltpeter, china-clay, borax and salt-marsh workings.

In emancipating himself, however, Patiño was no better nor worse than the thousands of mixed-blooded Bolivians who even today deny the obvious fact that they are related in any way to the Quechuas. Some have "passed over" completely to the white group in lands where their ancestry is not known. Some *cholos* who became wealthy fled to Europe and never returned to their native land; and in Bolivia, those who attained positions of authority over pure Quechuas became the most disdainful taskmasters. *Cholo* politicians and small office holders in Bolivia are the most offensive. They lose no opportunity to deceive, cheat and insult their lowlier kinsmen.

Patiño had raised himself into the middle class, but he was still a long way from the top. The handful of whites in Cochabamba's 22,000 population looked upon both *mestizos* and Quechuas with little more than toleration. They conducted business with the half-breeds out of necessity, but they did not accept any one of them as a social equal. Only a few white men even spoke to their *mestizo* acquaintances on the street, and all whites ignored the barefooted Quechuas completely.

The aristocrats of Cochabamba had long ago retired behind the locked doors of such institutions as the Club Social, the most exclusive in all Bolivia. The club's building became the symbol of white snobbery, and the only half-breeds who ever crossed its sacred threshold were servants.

In his new state of social consciousness, Patiño found himself drawn irresistibly to this citadel of race supremacy. Strolling every afternoon with Albina, he found enjoyment in fishing from the banks of the Rio Rocha, sitting on benches in the Plaza Colón, or walking through the Alameda. But on every walk he led Albina past the Club Social, sometimes several times a day. In only a few days, his sense of importance had become incredibly overweening and now he had decided that he would do the absolutely impossible—become a member of the Club Social.

The new and flattering greetings of "Don Simon," which he heard now on every side, may have put the idea in his head. At the least, the Spanish title gave him a warm glow and he soon began to rack his brains for a genealogical excuse to give the appellation more than an honorary justification. An anecdote often repeated in Bolivia says that he stumbled upon the answer by accident.

According to this story, a group of fawning *cholos* were talking to him one day about his trips to the Uncias.

"We thought for a while that you were crazy," one remarked, "but now we have changed our minds. You were merely lucky."

"Crazy?" Patiño protested. "Lucky? I was neither! I knew all the time exactly what I wanted."

"You knew about the tin?" an incredulous *cholo* demanded.

"Of course," Patiño boasted. "It has been my ambition since childhood, and I prepared myself for it. I have always studied mining. The Patiños have always been interested in mining. This is a rich land. Why shouldn't we?"

"The Patiños?" his questioner asked in surprise. "Are you related to *the* Patiños, the Conquistadores? The salt-marsh Patiño?"

This question gave Simon his chance. One of the early explorers of South America had been named Patiño. With other Spanish adventurers, he charted the Rio Pilcomayo, and one of the salty lakes on the river's banks was named in his honor. It is known today as the Esteros Patiño.

Answering the question, Patiño asserted boldly: "Of course, the salt-marsh Patiño was a member of my family."

Thus Patiño established his claim of relationship to one of the oldest names in South American colonization, to the Patiños who had settled in Peru centuries before, white Spaniards who aided Pizarro in his conquests. But Patiño ignored another line—the bronzed aboriginal kinsmen, the despised Quechuas. From that moment on, Patiño never admitted that these nameless Indian forebears were even twigs of his family tree.

Patiño was now white, all white, at least in his own opinion. The next time he passed the Club Social he viewed it exultantly, and he was actually convinced that he had made remarkable social progress. For the next twenty years he assailed its haughty walls fruitlessly, but in those first bright days in 1894, he could close his eyes and see upon the Club's roster: "Don Simon Iturri Patiño, scion of the Conquistadores."

Patiño Mining Enterprises is American company with American engineers, one of the most remarkable mines from engineering standpoint in world. Mining engineer Herbert Hoover probably never planned or dreamed of mine on such a scale. Located thousands of feet above sea level; all food, tools, water carried hundreds of miles from sea to top of mountain, scene of operations.—From a cabled report by an American correspondent.

9

El Minero Grande!

WHEN PATIÑO returned to La Salvadora at the head of a caravan of twenty-three mules, his passage through the lower heights of the Uncias signalized the return of industrial life to a region virtually dead in that respect.

Not since the Conquistadores had so formidable an expedition appeared. The persistent, greedy Spaniards had been rewarded in their frantic search for a city of gold by discovering one of the richest silver veins in the New World, located 16,000 feet high in the ribs of the Andes. The metal literally pushed itself from the ground, and wherever Indian slaves dug into the hills, their masters were rewarded with new discoveries. The invaders established a camp and began active mining operations within a month. They named the site Cerro Rico (rich mountain) and from its bowels they stripped sufficient silver to outfit the Spanish Armada of Philip II.

Operations spread a few kilometers away to Potosí, which in a quarter-century grew to be a city of 200,000 people, most of them slaves, toiling for King Philip. As a mark of his royal favor, Philip bestowed upon Potosí the title of "Royal Imperial City." For nearly four centuries, train after train of llamas and human freight bearers trudged back and forth from Potosí to the Pacific, down a tortuous thousand-mile trail, to load the ore on Spanish caravels and other ships awaiting cargoes in the Peruvian port of Mollendo. The bones of human and animal victims marked this route of greed. More than a million persons died to enrich the Spanish king.

After four centuries, however, the mines were apparently worked out, and the "Royal Imperial City" became almost a ghost town. Its great cathedral fell into ruins and was converted into a movie theater. The Spaniards ultimately deserted Potosí, and today its population of 20,000 is composed of the half-breed descendants of surviving slaves.

These inhabitants, and the Quechuas in the surrounding area, were justifiably astounded when they sighted Patiño's heavily laden pack train, kicking up a serpentine blanket of yellow dust, reminiscent of the golden days. The mules were weighted down with canned beans, dynamite, picks, shovels, hammers and bags of coca leaves. Thirty barefoot Quechuas, lured by wages of six cents a day and ample allotments of coca, accompanied Patiño.

The equipment Patiño brought to mine his tin indicated the general ignorance of tin-mining methods in Bolivia at that time. His first ore crusher was an enormous stone "wheel." The weight was hollowed in the center, slipped through a long upright pole and dropped back and forth upon the rich concentrates carefully placed under it by the peon labor. Patiño had worked out the details of this contraption with Albina's help. It served its purpose. Only three months after he set up a permanent camp atop Salvadora, Patiño had enough tin to warrant a delivery to Cochabamba.

Albina, who had gone to live with relatives in the city of Oruro, was ready to welcome her husband when he returned triumphantly with his first load of tin. Patiño did not bring all the ore his Indians had mined. More than half his mules had died during the descent and their cargoes were cached along the trail, wherever the animals had fallen victim to the deadly altitude sickness.

"You have learned a lesson," Albina told him. "From now on we will use llamas. They will carry less but they will last longer."

Patiño's first sale consisted of forty quintals of concentrates, or about two tons of metallic tin. It brought in cash a total of $700. Patiño was elated. The profit was enormous, in comparison to his expenses. His books showed that in wages he had expended less than $1.80 per day for all his thirty workmen, and part of that he had recovered through the sale of food and coca. All the Indians were now in debt to Patiño, who had established his first company store without delay.

The store cast shackles upon the men, as surely in 1894 as it does today. Patiño extended credit freely because he discovered quickly that a debtor worker is a permanent worker. The system was devastating and extremely effective. His Indians were never out of debt from the day they started work. Their children were born into debt and in debt they died.

On his next trip to Cochabamba, Patiño led 120 Quechuas and a train of ninety llamas. In three months' work at La Salvadora, he had made more money than he could have made in three years working for Frick.

Slowly, irresistibly, Patiño's camps in the heights grew larger and larger, and the increasing number of their fires lighted up the skies with reflections visible for many kilometers. In time there were thousands of these fires, producing a radiance plainly visible even in far away Oruro.

On every trip to Cochabamba, Patiño contracted new workers to add to his growing army, and at the same time bought additional llamas to bring out the rich freight and carry in profitable merchandise. His remarkable talent for expansion was obvious from the outset of his career. Every penny he earned, above a small amount necessary to keep Albina in food and lodging, was spent for new equipment.

In the first two years of his labors, Patiño followed the original tin vein down 250 feet into the mountainside, opened up twenty-one new veins, paid off the $5,000 mortgage, purchased 400 llamas, and employed 800 Quechua laborers. The workers' women soon joined their husbands, and Patiño lost no time in persuading them to work beside their husbands. He was delighted when the women showed a particular talent for sorting ore, and for the next half-century he employed them at this and other jobs. In 1933, during a manpower shortage caused by the Chaco War, Patiño actually ordered women into the deep pits to do the heavy, killing work of male drillers.

As the fires on the hills around Patiño's workings lighted the skies and attested a growing community, they also attracted attention to the little man's rapid financial success. Jealous Cochabambites soon were setting up tin mining companies of their own. In Patiño's example there was abundant evidence that silver was a thing of the past, that a ready cash market existed in their own town for all the tin that could be delivered. Prospectors swarmed through the Andes in search of new claims. A Chilean syndicate began operations on acreage four kilometers down the slopes from La Salvadora, and imported hundreds of Chilean miners to drill into the peak's heart. Criminals plotted to steal Patiño's claim, and bands of furtive gangsters even attempted his assassination. Several times he narrowly escaped death when snipers fired at him from behind the concealing crags.

Patiño's most exciting battles, however, were fought thousands of feet underground. They came when the Chilean mine owners pushed through a tunnel to invade his own workings. By this time, Patiño possessed a small arsenal, and with a picked group of armed laborers he fought his rivals back into their own corridors. Leading his little army in the darkness, with a German pistol in one hand and a *yareta* torch in the other, firing as he charged, Patiño won the temporary title of General for his bravery. After the battle, with many dead and wounded on both sides, the tunnel was sealed and a truce arranged, pending arbitration. Later the Chileans agreed to drive their tunnels in directions which would not puncture the walls of the Salvadora galleries.

These clashes taught Patiño a lesson which he never forgot, and probably gave him the idea of preventing a recurrence by buying additional claims all over Bolivia so that he could curtail competition. The responsibility for supervising these new claims was assumed by Albina. While Patiño directed the work at La Salvadora, Albina sent scouts through the rich mineral belt, buying every likely claim offered for sale, and although she had an unshakable faith in tin, she did not overlook other metals. When Patiño took an inventory of his holdings, acquired during the first thirty-six months of Albina's activities, he found himself the owner of salt marshes, silver, gold, saltpeter, borax, emerald, malachite, tungsten, wolfram, lead, zinc, copper, platinum, bismuth, iron, mercury, manganese, alabaster, porphyry, cobalt, asbestos, opal, lapis-lazuli and China clay deposits, with a few marble quarries thrown in.

During two of those three years, Albina had also presented her husband with two other treasures, his first-born children: a son, Antenor, and a daughter, Elena.

At the end of those three years, Patiño was unable to arrive at any accurate estimate of his wealth. He had only a small sum of cash on hand, scarcely enough to continue his mining operations, but in properties he was a potential millionaire. Of all the mineral claims his wife had sought, only one remained outside his grasp. It was the one operated by the Chileans near his precious Salvadora, and he vowed that some day he would have that claim too. The mine was called Llallagua, and there was only one thing that Patiño wanted more—membership in the Club Social.

There was certainly no other fly in Patiño's rich ointment. His properties had become world-famous. Although it was still worked by the most primitive methods, La Salvadora was known in England, Germany, Malaya and the United States as a proved mine of almost fabulous value. The bandits of Bolivia were far from being the only men who looked at it with acquisitive eyes. Europeans played with the thought of buying it, but American miners were the first to make a definite proposal.

It was the representatives of the Leeds tin plate empire who came within a breath of purchasing La Salvadora at a time when Patiño was desperately short of operating capital. Leeds' emissaries sailed from New York to Buenos Aires, and made the perilous trip to Cochabamba by train, on foot and on muleback to tempt the little man with more money than he had ever dreamed of possessing, even from La Salvadora's enormous profits. But once more fate and Albina teamed up to save him.

When Leeds' men finally reached Patiño's camp, they arrived on the only day that Albina had visited there since she and her husband had first come to the mine. Albina was napping in Patiño's bedroom when the Yankee visitors rapped on his adjoining office door. The Spanish-speaking American engineers, tired from the long trip and anxious to get back to civilization, got down to business in a hurry.

"Señor Patiño," said the spokesman, "we are not here to dicker. Frankly, we wish to buy your mine. We have a trading price and a top price."

Patiño's eyes narrowed. He had scarcely enough cash on hand to meet the monthly payroll. All of his new ore was earmarked for equipment debts in Cochabamba and Oruro.

"I am not interested in your trading price," Patiño said baldly. "What is your offer? Your top offer?"

"The sum of $300,000 in cash—gold dollars—a million bolivianos."

Patiño swallowed hard and struggled to hide his astonishment. This incredible sum was twice as much as he believed any combination of miners would possibly offer for his property. At that moment he decided to sell La Salvadora, but his native shrewdness stopped from jumping at the first offer.

"I do not wish to sell at that price," Patiño said. "The

Germans have already offered an identical sum. I am holding out for dollars 350,000."

The Americans demurred.

"I tell you that we have a top price," the spokesman said. "We cannot raise it. We have made you a generous offer, more than the property is actually worth."

"I am holding out for dollars 350,000," Patiño insisted.

At either figure, Patiño thought, he would be the richest man in Bolivia, and Albina would be overjoyed when he told her that they could live in luxury for the rest of their lives.

Another engineer spoke: "Our agents have made a careful survey of your mines, Señor Patiño. We are convinced that your ore reserves are only 56,000 tons. Three hundred and fifty thousand dollars is actually far too much for any sensible firm to pay. But we have our orders."

"Dollars 350,000," Patiño repeated stubbornly. "That and no less."

The Leeds men asked Patiño for a few minutes to consider. They went outside and conferred for nearly an hour in loud whispers. The time consumed in this conference was their undoing, for when they finally returned to tell Patiño that his terms would be accepted, Albina stirred restlessly and woke up.

"We have prepared a written agreement," the spokesman said. "All that is necessary is to fill in the sum."

The man reached for a pen on Patiño's crude table

desk and wrote out the terms of the transaction, then signed it in behalf of his corporation. Patiño's hand trembled as he reached for the bill of sale. The visitor passed him the pen. Patiño read the document because he thought that was the thing to do, although actually he was not concerned with its conditions and stipulations. He felt that he had driven a shrewd bargain and outsmarted the Yankee engineers in a masterful display of business acumen.

"It seems satisfactory," Patiño said. The little miner began writing his name, and had scribbled "Simo—" when the door opened and Albina stepped into the room.

"What are you doing?" she demanded suspiciously. She stared at the pen in Patiño's hand and regarded the visitors appraisingly.

"Albina, I have wonderful news!" Patiño blurted. "I am selling La Salvadora for dollars 350,000. We will be the richest of all Bolivians."

For reply, Albina lunged toward the desk, knocked the pen out of Patiño's hand, grasped the bill of sale and tore it into shreds before the eyes of the startled Americans.

"Fool," she screamed, "selling our mine!"

"But there are only 56,000 tons in reserve," Patiño protested, almost pitifully. "It is a good price!"

"We will go bankrupt with La Salvadora," Albina shouted, "or you will become *el gran minero!* La Salvadora has a million tons of tin!"

Albina's estimate of La Salvadora's tin reserve was

certainly more accurate than that of the frustrated American engineers. More than 300,000 tons have been produced by La Salvadora, and it is estimated conservatively that the mine contains several times that amount in its forty-six main veins and one thousand branches. More than 100,000 tons are blocked out at the present time.

After the Leeds men left, Albina gave her husband a thorough lacing down. She chided him for his lack of faith, and when he protested that cash was short, she is said to have replied: "We borrowed five thousand dollars when we had only a shallow tunnel. Now we possess a mine. We will mortgage La Salvadora once more, but this time for real money. We must have modern equipment."

A few weeks later, Patiño was able to negotiate a large loan from a group of British bankers in Oruro and Cochabamba. It was a sum reported to be more than $200,000. With it Patiño was able to begin the first step of his mechanical expansion. New type motors, given the name *motors electricos Patiños,* were manufactured by German engineers especially for the peculiar mining requirements of La Salvadora. They were designed to operate efficiently in high altitudes.

Little by little, Patiño imported the most modern technical equipment from Europe, as well as heavy machinery from the United States. His production spurted. He organized the Empress Minera la Salvadora, and in a few short years he was rolling in riches. So rapidly did his new methods produce tin concentrates that he was able shortly to overcome one of his most perplexing problems, that of transportation. He required desperately a railroad to connect the mine at Uncia with the terminus of a line which ended at Machacamarca. It would take 120 miles of track to join with the main railroad running from Oruro to the Pacific port of Antofagasta. Patiño asked his wife's advice. He was worried.

"It would take all of our money," he told Albina.

"Build it anyway," Albina ordered. "We need it to bring in machinery and take out ore. It will pay for itself."

Hesitantly Patiño awarded contracts for the biggest undertaking of his life. When the railroad was ultimately completed, he had spent nearly six million dollars in gold in its construction.

Before the last spike was driven and the station completed at Uncia, Albina had presented her husband with two more members of their family. The third child was a son, Rene, and the fourth was a daughter, Graziela. Patiño was so occupied with his work that he was almost a stranger to his first two children. While other successful miners indulged themselves and their families with luxurious trips to Europe and the Orient, Patiño had assiduously applied himself to supervising every minute detail of his operations. No other industrialist in Bolivia could boast of a fortune so large, or properties of comparable scope.

Craftily, Patiño branched out on his own with new

companies. He obtained remarkable concessions from the Bolivian government, through political and economic influence. He bought the Compania Minera de Uncia, a mine adjacent to his own property, and bought into scores of other Bolivian industries. To finance his new ventures, he founded in Oruro the Banco Mercantil, and later opened branches not only all over the Republic of Bolivia, but also in the Chilean port of Antofagasta. Now a full-fledged banker as well as a miner, Patiño obtained cash from his own financial institutions under more favorable conditions than he had ever enjoyed.

His banks rapidly became the most powerful financial organizations in South America. Through his doors streamed thousands of industrialists who found themselves in financial straits. Every venture Patiño undertook met with fantastic success. Mining claims which had been considered worthless became fabulous producers almost overnight. Silver pits abandoned by British, German and Bolivian engineers were reopened by Patiño's workers, who soon discovered undreamed-of riches in hidden veins.

Patiño founded the first electric power and light enterprise in his district. He electrified the city of Oruro, and later headed a new syndicate to modernize and electrify the Bolivian capital of Sucre. With uncanny judgment, he bought from British interests the great mines of Huanini and Japo, which were failing, and converted them into highly profitable properties within a few months.

Although Patiño is credited with "generous and timely" assistance to failing Bolivian enterprises, he invariably at a later date acquired complete control over every distressed business he undertook to save. For example, he "saved" the Cochabamba Electric Light and Power Company from failure, but he soon owned 100 per cent of its stock.

At an early date Patiño recognized the potential petroleum industry in his country and organized the Sucre Sociedad, which rapidly acquired every likely deposit in the province of Acero. Patiño had been joined in this enterprise by associates, but the organization showed signs of failing and he was able to obtain complete ownership of the business. After that, he began to realize enormous profits from the operations. One after another, Patiño brought within his grasp dozens of shaky corporations. Through third parties, he bought the rich Kami wolfram deposits in the department of Cochabamba and developed them into one of the richest producers in the world. At the same time, he reopened the abandoned Conquechaca mines, which had been inundated, and recaptured them through the use of British and German pumps which he later utilized to equip a mammoth electric plant at Puculco Falls.

Patiño's appetite for wealth and power was insatiable. He even acquired the alcohol monopoly of his country through political machinations, and has derived an enormous profit from it ever since.

But Patiño never lost sight of tin, even as he never

forgot that Albina was to be consulted at every new step he took in his business. Tin was his first love, and he bought new deposits of enormous value. One was the great Luco Grande mine near Potosí, another the Luco Chico in the same department. His agents and banks grabbed other mines at Calquiri and Aroca. Patiño purchased a dozen gold mines as far away as the department of La Paz, and set about the development of his bismuth and antimony mines on a colossal scale.

In his spongelike absorption of Bolivia, Patiño bought up millions of acres of the richest farms, constructed artificial lakes to supply his hydro-electric plants, and brought in hundreds of foreign engineers to keep his machinery in order and draw up plans for even bigger operations.

"Patiño buildings" dotted every city of importance in the country. These structures were devoted to banking, merchandising and import-export ventures. He bought into steamship companies, including many operated by Chilean, Argentine, Dutch and British lines.

In a few years, La Salvadora was producing 2,500 tons of tin per day. The great plant's machinery was operated by Diesel engines and hydro-electric machinery which consumed 30,000,000 kilowatt hours a year.

All these things Patiño accomplished in the opening years of this century. Once he got started, the pieces of his fabulous empire fell into place with amazing speed, and in an incredibly short time the whole picture of wealth and power was complete. What happened after this opening phase of his life was simply an enlargement of that picture until it covered the globe.

Shortly after the turn of the century, the enlargement process began. It began with a vacation, the first one Patiño ever had, which originated on the day Patiño went to visit Albina in one of his early mansions, named Villa Albina in her honor. On that occasion he scarcely recognized his oldest son, whom he had not seen for many months. He spoke of this to Albina.

"You are very rich, Simon," his wife said. "Millions have come to you faster than to any other man, and it is now time for you to cultivate your family. We should take a trip."

The thought of a trip excited Patiño, but his answer was typical.

"If I could only make it pay," he lamented.

"You can," Albina assured him. "We can go to Germany."

The farsighted Albina was thinking of the great new fortune to be made if Patiño could learn from the Germans how to smelt his own tin.

The Tin King had never been outside his native country when he found himself the owner of a score of industries, which proves that one can learn between Cochabamba and Oruro what others may not learn traveling from Pole to Pole.—From an article in The Pan American Magazine.

10

"Now You Are Victoria!"

WHEN PATIÑO crossed the Argentine border, according to a Patiño legend that has never been verified, it was the first time he had ever been outside his native Bolivia. Buenos Aires itself overwhelmed him with its cosmopolitan magnificence, but the city might well have been taken aback by the opulence of Patiño's entourage. It included his wife and their four children, eleven relatives (mostly cousins), five nurses, two chefs, eight valets, three secretaries and a bookkeeper.

The Patiño caravan would have been impressive enough by itself, but it also included a group of native farmers and cattlemen who drove before them through the streets of the Argentine capital a dozen fat cows and steers, and carried coops on their shoulders filled with chickens, guinea hens and several armadillos. Others were loaded down with sacks of flour, packages of coffee, tea, salt and pepper, cooking utensils and every conceivable staple item of food a housewife would find necessary to use in a kitchen.

The lowing of the livestock, the cackling of the chickens, and the calls of the guinea hens in the incongruous setting of Buenos Aires' fashionable streets startled many a pedestrian, especially when they sighted Patiño and his retinue leading the procession.

At the gangplank of the transatlantic boat, he was challenged by a purser whose eyes popped in astonishment. The purser was even more amazed when he discovered that this little man was the gentleman who had booked fully one-half of the big liner's cabins.

"What is the meaning of the animals and fowls, Señor Patiño?" he inquired in bewilderment.

"Why, I understood it was a long voyage to Germany," Patiño replied.

"So it is," said the purser, "but still I do not understand."

"We have to eat, do we not?" Patiño demanded, somewhat petulantly. "I have a big party, as you can see. My children will need milk, so I have brought milk cows. We will need meat, so I have brought steers to be slaughtered during the voyage. We will need a variety in our diet, so I have chickens, guinea hens, and armadillos for steaks."

The purser thereupon enlightened the naïve traveler on the facilities of modern ocean vessels. "You will not even need your chefs," he added. "We carry numerous cooks, waiters and all standard types of servants to attend to your every need."

Patiño agreed, reluctantly, to send the livestock back to the markets, but he insisted that all of his employees accompany him, as originally planned. Later, an arrangement was made for his native chefs to prepare all the meals for the Patiño suites in the Patiño manner. The ship's officers could scarcely refuse even such an unusual request as the loan of the ship's kitchen, when the requester was a man who bought a hundred staterooms for a crossing when he actually needed not many more than twenty.

This particular part of the Patiño legend also asserts that the little man was never completely convinced that the vessel carried food until he saw the first meal. Then he sighed in a relieved way, and settled down to enjoy the voyage.

His fellow passengers settled down to enjoy Patiño and his party, a strange collection of poncho-clad men and women pattering about the ship's decks in leather sandals. When Patiño and Albina visited the main salons, a distinguished-looking passenger stared at them curiously on several occasions, and at last approached the miner one afternoon and asked if he might make a sketch of his face.

"It is a very interesting face," the stranger remarked, "and it would give me pleasure to sketch it for you."

"Go ahead," Patiño grunted. "I have nothing to lose."

The stranger smiled and proceeded to draw his subject with a set of charcoal pencils which he produced from a pocket. He worked rapidly and finished the sketch in a few minutes, after which he walked over and presented it to the restless Patiño.

"Here you are," he said politely. "It is a present for you. I hope you like it."

Patiño glanced indifferently at the drawing, stuffed it in his inside coat pocket, and promptly forgot the incident. The ship's captain mentioned the episode later, when he was showing Patiño the engine room.

"By the way," the captain remarked, "do you know the man who did your drawing the other day?"

"No, I do not know this man," Patiño said.

"Well, he is the famous tenor, Enrico Caruso," the captain told him. "Don't you know that he appeared at the Teatro Colón in Buenos Aires? If you will excuse me, I cannot understand why you are not impressed by the honor he paid you."

"Tenor? Tenor, you say?" Patiño's voice was scornful. "Well, I have enough money to make him *dance* for me if I wish it."

The lazy days aboard ship gave Patiño and Albina uninterrupted hours to plan one of the most important and daring steps in his career, the acquisition of a smelting industry. Patiño had never been satisfied with the profits from tin mining alone after he found out that others were enriching themselves through the smelting of his metal. The angry thought occurred to him every time he watched a llama train, or the flat cars that came later, transporting cargoes down to the Chilean port.

Before the liner reached Hamburg, Patiño and his wife had devised a plot for a tin monopoly which would give him control of the metal from the time it was lifted out of the earth until it was transmuted into its many commercial forms. Then and there he formulated the slogan: "From ore to tin can."

One of the most important stages between the concentrates and the refined product was the smelter. Tin's refractory nature had made a failure of electric furnace smelting in Chile and Bolivia. The absence of fuel in Bolivia and its scarcity in other South American countries had prevented the establishment of successful large-scale plants anywhere on the continent. In the early days of Patiño's career, most of his tin was shipped to German smelters which long before had been constructed to process the ore from mines in Saxony and Bohemia.

From the outset of his mining activities, Patiño had been a friend and admirer of the Germans. At one time he had planned with German capitalists a great railroad line from the city of Alto, Peru, to a port on the Rio Marmore, a branch of the Amazon. The Germans spent millions of pounds sterling on preliminary surveys, but the project was abandoned. Patiño, however, was most pleased with what he called the "sportsmanship" of the Germans, who paid all the losses. Under the agreement he would have shared equally with his German associates in the profits, but the failure had not cost him a cent.

Now, as a logical consequence, he turned to these "wonderful people" to discuss his smelting ambitions. All his business relations with them had been profitable and therefore pleasant. Their ready market for his tin had made it possible for him to change his diet from canned beans and sun-dried *charqui* meat to delicacies only a millionaire could afford. German money had enabled him to move out of a miserable hut of rough stones built over a muddy floor, and into a splendid mansion. The Germans, he considered, were his lucky race.

Moreover, German mechanical talent had already played a large role in the drama of his success. Hamburg engineers devised his machinery and milling methods, showed him how to make rich concentrates by mixing the ore with sulphide minerals, taught him the gravity method of concentration. He adopted their suggestions for calcining processes and flotation methods to eliminate sulphur and arsenic. The engineers installed magnetic separators to take out the iron; and before Patiño could afford expensive equipment they constructed makeshift hand-sorting belts which were jiggled and sprayed simultaneously with jets of water as the ore passed, to form concentrates. To German genius, Patiño owed the utilization of women ore pickers and sorters. German inventors even produced a specially designed hammer for Patiño's female workers to break up large lumps of ore into small fragments.

To one German mining engineer, Patiño owed as much as to any other man in his experience with La Salvadora. He had once been tempted to sell the mine, even before the Leeds representatives appeared, but this engineer had advised him against it.

"We are running into poor veins everywhere we tunnel," Patiño protested. "Maybe this is the time to unload all of it. La Salvadora is running out."

"Be patient," the German advised him. "You will see."

Shortly after, laborers followed the low-grade vein which had so discouraged Patiño a few hundred yards deeper into the mountainside. It opened up into fabulously rich workings.

But in spite of his enormous debt to the Germans, and his strong liking for them, Patiño repaid them when he got to Hamburg by ruining those who had been his best friends. It came about almost by accident, when the little Bolivian visitor learned soon after his arrival that the tin mines in Saxony and Bohemia were running out. To his further astonishment, he discovered that the Essen plant which had smeltered his ore for several years would have had to close down if it did not have his tin. The Essen contract was due to expire in a few weeks.

Patiño whistled when he added up these fortunate circumstances. Albina had been right. The trip would pay for itself a thousand times over if things turned out well.

Concealing his excitement, he met with representatives of the Essen plant and offered to buy their smelter. He named a price so low that the owners laughed in good-natured amusement. They were alarmed and angered a moment later when Patiño casually remarked: "It is too bad about the Saxony and Bohemia mines."

"What about them?" the Germans asked quickly.

"Only that my contract to supply you with ore unfortunately is expiring at the same time the German mines are expiring."

"But you will renew, won't you, Señor Patiño?" an anxious executive asked.

"No, I don't think so," Patiño told him bluntly. "You see, I would like to buy your smelter. Otherwise, I plan to sell my ore to the British."

The Germans were completely at his mercy. They knew Patiño's threat was good, that without his ore their smelters would be worthless. Patiño got the smelter at his own, mercilessly low price.

Yes, Patiño reflected afterward, the Germans were wonderful people.

This deal was only the starting point in Patiño's conspiracy. He planned to buy every important tin smelter in the world. Greatest of all was the enormous Williams, Harvey & Co. smelter at Bootle, England, near Liverpool. It was several years later, however, before the opportunity came for him to buy into this huge operation.

The entering wedge to the English firm proved to be Edward Joel Cornish, president of the three-hundred-million-dollar National Lead Company, which consumed more tin than any other company in the world, with the exception of the United States Steel Corporation. Without Patiño's tin, Cornish knew he would not be able to write the fat dividend checks which had made his corporation one of the most profitable in the history of American big business. Conversely, Patiño found in National Lead a steady, reliable customer for all the tin his mines could produce.

These two utterly diverse men—the corn-fed Iowa boy and the Bolivian half-breed—were brought together by Frank Pearce, British manager of Williams, Harvey & Co. At the suggestion of Pearce himself, they became his partners in the great Bootle smelter. The combination was unbeatable.

Patiño had another reason for making this deal, other than the building of a monopoly. He had decided that Germany was preparing for war, and that she would inevitably break with England. The resulting conflict would jeopardize his Essen smelting operations. He was playing safe, therefore, by making the English deal. No matter which side won, he would have at least one smelter in a victorious country and his mining operations in Bolivia would not be interrupted.

There was still another ramification. Patiño thought he could use Cornish to wrest the Llallagua mine adjoining La Salvadora away from its Chilean owners. Llallagua, the only non-Patiño mining property of any consequence in Bolivia, had always been coveted by the little man, besides which there was his personal score to settle against the hated Chileans, whom he had fought so bitterly when he was developing La Salvadora. The Chileans, however, had been as stubborn and vindictive as Patiño. They had rejected derisively every buying overture. What Patiño needed was a powerful American ally, a man rich in cash and prestige to act as a secret agent in the purchase of the property. Cornish, he decided, was his man.

Once the decision was made, Patiño packed his bags and made a hurried trip to New York, where he met with Cornish and the directors of National Lead at their offices, 111 Broadway. Patiño made his proposition bluntly.

"Señors," he said, "I want your help."

Then he outlined his plan, by which National Lead would buy Lllallagua for him. Cornish and the directors hesitated.

"It will cost only $1,500,000," the Bolivian reassured them.

No, it was not the question of money that was troubling them, the directors replied. It was a matter of policy, a question of whether the manufacturer should become the miner. The manufacturer had already broken a precedent by becoming a smelter. This further step was something they would have to think over.

Patiño left the meeting in anger and bought his return ticket to Bolivia. When he was only three days out of New York on the way home, a wireless informed him that National Lead had decided to go along with him. Soon after, the company's agents bought Llallagua, and Patiño became the owner of the entire mountain. When the papers had been signed, he took Albina and together they walked to the main shaft of the mine he had coveted for so long. Cupping his hands, Patiño shouted triumphantly into the yawning hole:

"You are no longer Llallagua. Now you are Victoria."

Only Patiño would have thought of that gesture.

Patiño went back to Oruro to live and built a lovely house, the first of his palaces. Soon after he went to Paris—for no reason except that he liked the French way of life, the luxury, the comfort.—From a report by an American correspondent.

11

The Exile

WHEN PATIÑO screamed into Llallagua's chasm, he felt that he had reached a milestone in his life. He had always hated the Chileans for very Patiño-like reasons—because Bolivia had lost her Pacific ports to Chile, and any Chilean who reaped a profit from the resources of Bolivia was a man to be despised, and Patiño had suffered more than any other Bolivian from this state of affairs. Consequently it was an enormous satisfaction to him when he restored Llallagua to Bolivian ownership, particularly *his* ownership. He felt suddenly more free.

This freedom consisted primarily of turning his full attention to the rounding out of his empire, and of his personal life. That meant, first, satisfying his appetite for expansion; and second, fulfilling his almost pathetic yearning for social recognition. Patiño had never wavered from his great ambition to achieve membership in the Club Social. To the white Brahmins of the Social, he was still a *cholo*.

The expansion came first by necessity, because Patiño was completely involved with his huge operations, obligations and commitments of every kind, but it came first at this particular time in a way he had not foreseen. The truth was that Patiño had expanded himself to the point of bursting, like a giant balloon.

Bolivia had discovered that Patiño's exploitation of tin was her most important single source of income, consequently the little man's political power had reached a height never before enjoyed by any Bolivian civilian; he had become synonymous with Bolivia. Reluctantly Patiño was forced to admit the costly fact that Bolivia's economy was as vital to him as his own. Only by paying higher and higher taxes could he keep his country from anarchy.

Further, his cash reserves were now dangerously low. Expansion had carried his industrial activities over the globe. He had bought into properties in Africa and Malaya, Czechoslovakia, Portugal, Spain and Indo-China. With the war clouds hanging ominously over Europe, the price of tin fell hourly and the future of his Essen smelter looked anything but hopeful. To complete the picture of his troubles, Patiño heard from New York and London that Cornish was quietly buying control of Williams, Harvey & Co.

Without huge new loans, the little man realized, he could not hold together his great empire, outsmart his associates and business rivals, and at the same time keep himself firmly entrenched. As always when he needed money, he turned to the British, and he decided on a hurried trip to London.

For the first time in his life Patiño acted without Albina's help. He sailed alone on his momentous voyage to Europe. At the time it appeared to him that he had brought disaster on himself by this act, for Germany and England went to war while his ship was still at sea, and the price of tin fell disastrously.

When he arrived in England, at the London board room of the Midland Bank of England he found a dismal lot of directors. Patiño was in the almost absurd position of applying for the biggest credit in his business career at a moment when the assets he proposed for security were almost worthless. The fourteen directors of the bank, which was already loaded down with Patiño tin collateral, told the Bolivian plainly that they had enough. In fact, they insisted that he pay all his old loans on the spot.

For the first time, Patiño was forced to stand alone in a time of great trouble. His only aide was an interpreter. Nonetheless, he argued his case stubbornly for hours. Over and over he insisted that England, in time of war, would need tin more than ever when the pressure for ordnance began. "Your nation," he predicted, "will be begging for my metal within six months."

Somehow, by this dogged reiteration, he accomplished the miracle. When Patiño left the board room, the directors had even absorbed some of the little man's eternal faith in the future of tin, and they had agreed to advance every cent he requested. True to his prediction, within a few months tin skyrocketed to $2,100 per ton. Gold poured into Patiño's coffers faster than it ever had before in his fantastic life.

Now he was able to do what he could not do before. One of his first steps was to buy, quietly, more of the Williams, Harvey & Co. stock, to forestall his old friend Cornish. At the same time his New York agents bought heavily into National Lead, and before the astounded gentleman from Iowa knew what was happening, Patiño not only controlled the Bootle smelter, but he was well on the way to domination of Cornish's own company.

Later, Patiño forced National Lead to sell all of its stock in the English company. At that time Cornish and Patiño clashed on the terms of the sale, and it was not consummated until the Bolivian, through Lehman Brothers of New York, launched his biggest financial undertaking on the New York Stock Exchange. The stock of Patiño mines and enterprises appeared on the Exchange's big board with a valuation of $29,000,000, and with a charter from Delaware. Cornish agreed to serve as vice-president of this company. Then came the final contest of wills. Patiño offered National Lead $105 per share for its Williams, Harvey & Co. stock.

"I would rather buy yours for $120 per share," Cornish countered.

Patiño's face hardened.

"You yourself told me not long ago that $70 per share was a fair price," he protested.

"There's a difference between buying and selling," the Iowan remarked calmly.

Finally the two men compromised, and Cornish gave in only after Patiño agreed to sign a ten-year contract with the English company for a fixed annual supply of his ore. Thus Cornish protected National Lead's own contract for tin with the Bootle smelter.

Patiño got his revenge a little later for not having had his own way. When Cornish asked him to pay for the stock with shares in Patiño mines and enterprises, Patiño insisted that the transaction be concluded "in cash." Cornish was so impressed by Patiño's evaluation of his own stock that he bought heavily into the company, big blocks of it at $26 per share. He continued to buy even when the stock began falling alarmingly. His buy orders were carried out until they reached a low of $12, at which point Cornish concluded his position was hopeless and sold out completely.

While all this was going on, Patiño's "Golden Age" had begun in earnest. Huge war profits and the unprecedented boom in all of his world-wide properties had relieved the financial strain. Patiño was now a billionaire in gold as well as in property deeds to the lucrative operations which produced it. His was not a paper fortune, like those of so many of the world's wealthy men.

In such a happy position, he could turn to the realization of his second great ambition: to be recognized socially. Money could buy this recognition, in part. The Bolivian gave the largest, most flamboyant entertainments the international set had ever seen, duly reported from a dozen capitals by the society writers. He acquired several magnificent yachts, and lived on them in Havana, the Mediterranean ports, and even farther away in Shanghai, Hongkong and other Far Eastern settings. Always he was surrounded by beautiful women, titled guests, social arbiters, spongers and hangers-on of every variety. The most lavish hosts on the Continent were taken aback by this magnificently empty display.

But the Cochabamba Club Social appeared unimpressed. The Patiño pomp had been fully reported on the front pages of Bolivian newspapers, but the accounts had not provoked an invitation to apply for the membership he so coveted.

Patiño decided that he would no longer try to crack the citadel by the display of his wealth. He would do it by diplomacy, literal and figurative. After talking it over with Albino, he ordered the Bolivian government to appoint him Minister to Paris. In this high office, he reasoned, the Club Social could scarcely refuse him membership, and at the same time—once more the characteristic Patiño reasoning—the appointment would be a stroke of business genius. It would cost the Bolivian treasury millions of dollars, because the position gave Patiño important tax exemptions, and similarly the French government could not levy its customary assessments on foreigners under international agreements exempting diplomats.

To mitigate the blow to the Bolivian government, Patiño announced that he intended to build at his own expense an impressive new Bolivian Ministry in Paris, and would pay its operational costs, including the salaries of its staff.

Arriving in Paris, the new diplomat bought a palace on the Avenue Foch, near the Bois de Boulogne. Decorators swarmed through its vaulted halls, main salons and dining rooms, ripping out masterpieces which had made it one of the most admired structures in Europe. The main ballroom, in authentic Louis XIV décor, was remodeled on Patiño's orders into something resembling a Moorish harem, which the little man had once seen and admired during his travels in North Africa.

"I also want a fountain placed in the middle of the floor," Patino ordered the bemused decorators. "It must have a stream so strong it will squirt to the ceiling."

A caravan of trucks carted away to warehouses scores of fine old fireplaces, rare tapestries, and tons of delicate copings and other fixtures which had once made this showplace the delight of connoisseurs. Other trucks brought in a weird collection of paintings in tin-and-gilt frames, and monstrosities of every sort, including a dozen five-ton glass chandeliers which were hung to replace crystal masterpieces. Patiño crammed the palace with Turkish, English and Moroccan "antiques," in an orgy of buying which left the French gasping at such extravagance. Naturally, the French art dealers were almost speechless with delight.

In this first year of his ministry, Patiño bought "masterpieces" by the gross and came to be known as the most genial collector who had ever indulged so expensive a hobby, by which accolade the French meant that he was the Gallic equivalent of a sucker. Stories of his collecting activities were cabled daily to Cochabamba and La Paz, but Patiño was also careful to see that the editors of his own Bolivian papers got other stories, with instructions that they be put on page one, outlining the details of his plan for an amazing palace in Cochabamba, the now famous architectural audacity to which he gave the name Miraflores.

Cochabambites also read, with falling jaws, of their countryman's purchase of villas and palaces all over Europe, and the construction on these properties of garages which now housed eighty-four Rolls-Royces and forty-three automobiles of American make, particularly Packards, Lincolns and Cadillacs. Patiño also bought horses, a hundred at a time, importing the best hunters from stables in England and Ireland. He purchased several fine stallions from the Aga Khan.

For three years Patiño lived in diplomatic magnificence in Paris and waypoints, waiting for the Club Social to absorb the fact that he was in his own estimation a most promising candidate for membership. When he thought the time was ripe, he prepared to return to Cochabamba and the elegance of Miraflores.

This home-town palace was now complete, an impressive evidence of his international fame. His son and daughters were accepted by the rich of nearly every country in the world, and he had cut a wide social swath on his own account. Patiño was the richest man in the world, but he felt it would mean nothing to him unless the Club Social took him in. He sailed from Cherbourg with the intention of applying for membership without waiting for an invitation.

All Bolivia knew of Patiño's homecoming. The newspapers proclaimed his royal progress, even those papers he did not own, because the Bolivian was news, whatever he did. Thirty French and English servants prepared Miraflores, and at last swung open the great bronze doors for the master's homecoming. Meanwhile, Patiño had mailed his application to the Club Social.

Unbelieving, and with the sharp stab of new frustration, Patiño read the dozen or so little cards that were delivered at Miraflores. They were written in the most formal manner, expressing regret that the senders were compelled by previous engagements to decline invitations to the series of splendid banquets Patiño had planned to celebrate the opening of his palace. All these correspondents were members of the Club Social. Patiño felt a cold wind down his spine, and his homecoming smile changed to a melancholy scowl.

This preliminary hint of the bitter truth was followed in a few days by a formal notice which he read aloud to Albina: "The membership committee of the Club Social regrets to advise the applicant, Simon Iturri Patiño, that his application presented at the last meeting of members received an unfavorable consideration."

In a monumental rage, Patiño fled Bolivia and never returned.

LA PAZ, Bolivia, April 13.—Cochabamba newspapers comment on the proposal of Simon I. Patiño to place $10,000,000 at the disposal of the Government for public works.

The works enumerated by Patiño are the construction of a highway between Cochabamba and Todos Los Santos, the establishment of a port at the junction of the rivers Chimore and Chapare, the canalizing of said rivers so as to facilitate access to the River Manore, and therefore to the Atlantic.

In exchange for uncultivated lands in Chapare, Patiño offers to colonize and industrialize that region. Patiño would grant extensive concessions in Isiboro, according to this plan.—New York Times, *April 14, 1928.*

12

"Hermit of Tin"

THE YEARS between the two World Wars completed the transition of Patiño from an acquirer of wealth to a user of wealth. That is, he grew richer by the minute, but his great fortune now became a political weapon.

When he returned to Paris after his self-exile from Bolivia, he soon established a reputation as a recluse, "the hermit of Tin," as Parisians called him. He stayed close to Albina, his children and his servants, except when he rode his horses along the bridle paths of the Bois, or motored on the boulevards of the capital.

Most of the time he was depressed. This depression was derived not only from his social failure, but from the world view he had acquired as the result of living abroad and of thinking his long, gloomy thoughts in seclusion. Patiño was aware of the changing social and economic structure of the world. He knew that the pattern which characterized his rise to power was ripping at the seams. Although he had come from the lowest of the lower classes, Patiño accurately if inconsistently put all the blame for the threatened change in the established order on the working people, the poor, whose increasing self-assertion he deplored.

Part of the little man's foresight was the result of his handling of an international empire that grew more fabulous as time went on. He had regained control of his German smelter, bought vineyards in Sicily, linoleum companies in France and England, and marble quarries in Belgium and Italy. Moreover, he had successfully carried out his plans to hold America in the grip of his smelting and tin monopoly by selling the tin market on the theory that only the British and Europeans could smelt his ore successfully, and that Bolivian ore was a low-grade product which had to be mixed with the ore from his African and Malayan mines to reach the proper perfection.

As the result of manipulating this far-flung empire, Patiño acquired a perspective that enabled him to anticipate the struggle for power which culminated in the second World War. The tin king may have seen the ideologies of fascism, communism and capitalism only in terms of his own financial structure, but his abnormally sharpened social consciousness made him almost the only industrialist in the twenties who fully sensed the underlying basis of conflict.

But business came first, always. Thus Patiño understood, and in a way appreciated, the adroit manner in which Adolf Hitler plunged Bolivia into a war with

Paraguay. While the world thought of this bloody affair only as a war between two small South American countries for an obscure piece of disputed territory lying between them, Patiño knew that the real object of the conflict was the ultimate building of a pipe line through the Chaco to the Atlantic Ocean, where Bolivian oil could then be pumped into Nazi tankers. He must have been aware of the impressive number of German officers in Bolivia at that time, and their domination of the Bolivian Army. His failure to do anything about it can only be considered as a tacit agreement.

One of the first Germans to be employed in Hitler's Bolivian plot was an ex-member of the Kaiser's staff, General Hans Kundt. Others of his caliber and background followed. There were also several high-ranking Nazis among those present in Bolivia, including Ernst Roehm, whose job was to drag the aboriginals out of the jungles, strip them of their blowguns and teach them how to use a Luger.

The Chaco War, in which Patiño backed the cause of National Socialism, lasted three years and cost the two countries involved more than 100,000 casualties. Paraguay's victory ended Hitler's scheme, and left Bolivia holding the bag, the contents of which was a loss of 100,000 square miles of territory and a bill for $194,000,000. By paying the bill through his companies' tax checks, Patiño became the only man in history to underwrite singlehandedly the entire cost of a nation's war.

While the war went on, Patiño followed its course by

daily cables in his Paris mansion. As his material contribution, he dispatched boatloads of British planes, artillery, grenades and ammunition to Bolivia, and he sent more and more German and even a few British military experts to bolster the Bolivian Army. Patiño has bitterly denied the statement published in various periodicals that some of this money came back to him in profits from a French munitions plant. The charge that he was part owner of the firm which sold arms impartially and brought him a profit out of his countrymen's blood, the tin magnate characterizes as a preposterous fiction. Nothing so annoys "patriota, numero uno."

After the Chaco War, Patiño did not drop National Socialism as an enterprise that had been, on the whole, unprofitable for him. He saw even more clearly than before that the greatest menace to his empire was communism, not only in its undiluted Russian form but in whatever variation of it appeared in the affairs of nations. It was natural, therefore, that Patiño should be a ready believer in the Hitler argument that National Socialism was the only hope of blocking the world ambitions of Moscow. When Spain became the first testing ground for this theory, Patiño took what most observers agree was an active part. He had been appointed Bolivian Minister to Spain during Franco's rise to power, and had moved his family to Madrid. Thereafter, according to numerous magazines and newspapers, he became the Falangist leader's principal backer in the struggle against the Republic. No one has ever proved this surmise, however, and it is virtually impossible to trace Patiño's movements during that period.

Franco's victory may have made Patiño feel slightly less gloomy about the state of things abroad, but concurrent affairs in his native Bolivia could only depress him anew. Bolivia had been left bankrupt by the Chaco War. Manpower shortages had reduced mining operations in every department. Revolution shook the nation. There were assassinations and the threat of anarchy, which alarmed the nation's neighbors even more than its leaders.

Patiño's major source of concern at home was the threatened nationalization of tin and other natural resources in order to save the muddled Bolivian economy. President German Busch suggested government seizure as the only means of saving his country, but he died under mysterious circumstances in the presidential palace at La Paz before his edict could be carried out. His death was announced officially as a suicide, but few informed South Americans doubted that he had been murdered by agents of nationalization's opponents. No one, however, accused Patiño.

There was still another thorn in Patiño's flesh. That was the rise of one Mauricio Hochschild, an Austrian-Jewish naturalized citizen of Argentina, whose antics in the tin market were first regarded as laughable and then were suddenly recognized as a real menace to Patiño's monopoly. Hochschild's genius appeared to lie in the development of properties which Patiño had considered too poor for profitable mining operations. The Argentinian was prevented from becoming a more serious menace only because of Patiño's international hold on smelting, a block which irritated Hochschild to the point where he constantly sought to embarrass Patiño. But the little man fought back ruthlessly, and meanwhile resolved to handle the upstart once and for all at some future date when he would be able to devote his talents to it.

Finally, in the catalog of Patiño's worries, there was the falling price of tin, foreshadowing the world glut which would end in abysmal depression.

In all this sea of trouble, the only island of satisfaction discernible to Simon Patiño's jaundiced eye was the news that a jury of Paris couturiers had nominated his daughter, Graziela, as one of the best-dressed women in Europe. She was down a trifle in the listing, not among the top ten, but when he recalled his Club Social snubbing, Patiño could not help feeling that the honor was a little triumph for him as well as Graziela. Momentarily, he glowed with pride.

To-day, it is difficult to imagine that, even among the uninstructed, there is anyone who does not regard the fall of commodity prices as the root cause of the present crisis.—Sir Henry Strakosch, in Fortune Magazine, *April, 1932.*

13

A Nail for Democracy's Coffin

In 1930, when the world was full of glum and bitter faces, there was no face more glum nor bitter than Simon Iturri Patiño's Bolivian countenance.

If he sailed in his yacht far offshore from Brazil's Matto Grosso, he could smell the acrid odor of once valuable coffee burning in dump heaps or belching pungently from locomotive smokestacks. If he went inland to São Paulo, Brazil's "Little Chicago," he saw only half-finished skyscrapers. The bitter reek of burned coffee hung over Patiño's native continent like the smell of doom—and in this case, doom could actually be said to have an odor.

As reports came in from Patiño's empire, he saw disaster no matter which way he looked. Red beans rotted on the trees from Mexico to the Argentine. Wheat prices tobogganed in the bread-baskets of the world. There was more wheat than the world had ever seen—billions of bushels rotting in elevators and bins—while the poor cried for bread. Similarly, sugar was piled in mountains on the docks and warehouse floors of Louisiana, Cuba and Florida, but little of it moved to fill the world's sweet tooth. The cotton farmers in Dixie, the long-staple growers in Egypt, and the planters of Brazil were in common peril.

Fitting the pieces together, Patiño could see that the world simply had more of everything than people could use. But when he sought the counsel of political leaders, the little man got only an official optimism that prosperity was just around the proverbial corner. In America, the dream of chickens in every pot and two cars in every garage died hard. In France, the hope for sauce Bordelaise on every table and picnics on the Marne for all suffered an even more lengthy strangulation.

Patiño's adopted nation could scarcely believe its eyes. The transplanted Bolivian observed gloomily that he could buy champagne for the old price of *vin ordinaire*, that the luxury liners on which he once sailed in elegance now held mostly third-class passengers, that centimes appeared on the roulette tables of Monte Carlo. Yet the French leaders assured him of the quick return of luscious escargots for all citizens, of rich cream from Normandy, of higher wages and a healthy economy.

As he anxiously scanned his world empire for some more substantial hope, Patiño was aware that the Japanese were still another threat to an economy of which he was a principal entrepreneur. The Japs dumped their cheap trash, manufactured by virtual slave labor, upon an already bankrupt world. They stole copyrights, and by naming a Japanese town "Sweden," were able to produce matches labeled "Made in Sweden," just as they had changed another Jap village to Usa (pronounced Ooser) for the production of tin cars "Made in U.S.A." Japanese trash merchandise covered the globe, ignoring international patents, and selling only because it was so cheap.

Patiño found, in his frantic survey of the world situation, that the thing he dreaded most was coming to pass. Depression advanced every variety of communism and it cropped out in every world capital in the actions of desperate men. To the tin king, these strikes and riots were no more foreboding than what he heard from the lips of the great statesmen. In his state of mind, it sounded like utter treachery for Britain's Prime Minister to declare at the World Economic Conference in London: "If we could restore the purchasing power of the nations which have been impoverished, and expand our resources by a greater employment of the people, we might in time get rid of the present excess of production and the menace of overproduction. In the meantime, however, we have to face the question of controlling production. . . . What, in the name of common sense, can anyone object to in a rational and well-thought-out scheme for limiting production in relation to the market demand?"

This idea, so contrary to Patiño's theory of economics, made the tin king shudder. He was profoundly frightened by what might conceivably happen to him; but even faced with the threat of cosmic collapse, he could also be annoyed by the relatively trivial fact that the depression had come at the moment of his greatest social triumph. His oldest son, Antenor, was soon to become the husband of the niece of the Bourbon and Catholic king of Spain. This event meant more to Patiño than any honor or wealth that he had acquired, more than all the medals on his fashionably cut vest of which he was so inordinately proud.

In this moment of mingled triumph and disaster, Patiño rubbed his medals and tried to figure things out. He stood to be the biggest loser in the world, simply because he had more to lose. His medals were symbolic of the eminence he had attained. They included the Grand Cross of the Order of Military Merit, Bolivia, in recognition of his services in the Chaco War; the Grand Cross of the Order of El Condor, Bolivia; the Grand Cross of the Order of the Holy Sepulcher; and the Grand Cross of the Order of Isabel la Catolica, Spain, conferred on him by the Spanish king himself in recognition of Patiño's efforts to bring about closer relations between their two countries.

As he fingered these symbols of his power, Patiño conceived of a plan to save himself. It was a plan of unbelievable magnitude. At the moment of its conception, Patiño was standing under a Gobelin tapestry in the library of his great villa in Biarritz, and in his excitement he stood up straight, stretched exultantly to his full five feet four inches, finished off the pint of champagne he held in his hand, laid aside his fine two-dollar cigar, and walked out of the room into a vaulted castle hall where his $100,000 El Grecos were hung. In a voice so loud that all his twenty-four servants could hear him, he shouted for Albina. Now, as he had from the beginning, he needed her at the moment of crisis.

When Albina came, the plan Patiño explained to her was simply one that would put teeth into an already existing tin cartel. This cartel, the Tin Producers Association, was formed in 1929, but it had turned out to be a clumsy, floundering, ineffectual combine, made so because of the differences in the problems of its members. For instance, the miners in Malaya and the dredgers in the Dutch East Indies had little in common with the lode miners of Bolivia, Australia, Siam, Africa and Indo-China, where production costs were nearly 300 per cent higher. The Malayans panned almost chemically pure ore for as little as $245 per ton, while the East Indians brought high-grade concentrates from pits at an even smaller cost. In all, there were nine producing countries represented in the tin organization, and the differences among them were so great that it was believed impossible to make the Association work.

But Patiño thought he had the answer. When he finished conferring with Albina in Biarritz, he ordered one of his six Rolls-Royce cars made ready for an emergency trip to Paris. Ten days later he stepped from a plane at Croydon in company with his son Antenor and a trusted aide, R. M. Vargas, and hurried to a fashionable town house at 7 Lygon Place, in London. In the next few hours the doors of the house admitted men of many races and colors, from Portugal, the Belgian Congo and Ruanda (Urundi), from French Indo-China, Malaya, the Dutch East Indies, Nigeria, Siam and Cornwall. Some were swarthy, some were fat and Dutch, some were yellow men and some brown, but all of them were rich with the riches of a metal that looked like moonlight on snow. Only China and a few other "outside" producers like Japan were not represented.

The 1930 meeting got under way when Sir Philip Cunliffe-Lister, a noted British industrial mediator, rapped his ivory gavel and called the group to order. Producers of 85 per cent of the world's tin were present in person, or were represented by a high dignitary, as in the case of Queen Wilhelmina of the Netherlands, whose emissary was the Governor-General from Batavia, Jan de Iongh. Every delegate to the meeting was important to tin: together they controlled an annual production of more than 130,000 tons.

In 1930, these tin operators had produced more than 170,000 tons for a world which normally used only 135,-000 to 150,000 tons. The biggest tin year of all had been 1929, when the production was 195,000 tons. In that same year the world used only 166,000 tons, a difference which accounted for at least part of the alarming "official" 61,000-ton surplus which now helped to depress prices still further. Since 1926 the world had consumed only 735,000 tons of tin, but it had produced nearly 825,000 tons.

An obvious discrepancy between the official surplus figure of 61,000 tons and the actual surplus of 115,000 tons indicated by figures quoted privately was simply ignored by the powerful tin merchants. Patiño and his fellows knew that such accurate information would not help the tin market, because tin had always been a sentimental commodity on the metal exchanges of the world, either supported with unreasoning enthusiasm by traders who were all bulls simultaneously, or dumped by the same men whenever they all became bears overnight. The tin barons had released the smaller figure, in all probability, to diminish the possibility of further panic selling.

The troubled gentlemen who gathered in Sir Philip's town house at Patiño's behest had always been compelled to deal with the most fantastic fluctuations of tin prices. In 1898, 130 million tons of tin at the high of 19 cents per pound would have sold for approximately $50,000,000; while in 1919, when the metal brought $1.10 per pound, it would have commanded nearly $300,000,000. The price got as low as 10 cents per pound in the years after the first World War, when in 1922, 130 million tons of tin were worth only $26,000,000. Thus, between 1926 and 1930, the producers lost annually about $100,000,000, based on the high of $1,400 per ton in 1926 and the low of $545 in 1930, when Patiño called the Association's members together.

It was an oddly met group of men that responded to Sir Philip's gavel that day in London. Some were suspicious, and all of them were at least partially puzzled. Only a few knew that Patiño was largely responsible for the meeting, but all of them were aware that the Bolivian represented one of their apparently insoluble "differences." Patiño's mining operations in Bolivia now stood to cause him a loss of approximately $24,000,000 annually, as against a profit of about the same amount only a few years before. His losses from mining operations outside his native country were in the same proportion, but the exact figures were a carefully guarded secret. In the four years between 1926 and 1930, it was estimated that Patiño's total losses would add up to about $150,000,000. The Malayans could continue to operate profitably even if tin dropped still lower. Malaya profits for 1930 were expected to be good, possibly as much as $10,000,000—not much compared with the bonanza years, of course, but still enough to make the Malayans unsympathetic about cooperating for the benefit of their Bolivian and African competitors.

This situation was typical of the Association's lack of cohesiveness, and it accounted for the puzzled curiosity of the members who gathered in Sir Philip's home.

The announced purpose of the meeting, when it came, created an uproar. Sir Philip gave the first hint when he cleared his throat nervously, and said: "Gentlemen, voluntary restriction of tin production is not the answer to our problems!"

In more direct words, Sir Philip was suggesting a cartel—plus!

Patiño looked around the room and studied the faces of the men. The low-cost Malayans looked apoplectic; the high-cost Malayans seemed pleased, as did the men representing high-cost Africa. The Dutch were poker-faced, the Portuguese smiling, the British almost as jubilant as the Siamese, whose problems were much the same. Patiño's long, thin mouth twisted a little. What he saw gave him some encouragement, but the most delicate stage of the meeting was still ahead.

Antenor shifted uncertainly in his chair. Vargas stared straight ahead. All three Bolivians knew that the fate of their nation's tin and of Patiño's profits depended on the success of the little man's plan, one which he had long since conveyed to the men who had engineered the meeting.

As Sir Philip unfolded this plan, he did not once by word or action intimate that it was solely Patiño's. He proposed it simply as a plan for the benefit of all.

"First," Sir Philip declared, "all tin-producing nations should be represented by a committee with authority to fix definite tin quotas, and the enforcement of these quotas shall be enforced by the various governments."

That last clause was Patiño's device to make the Association work, the "teeth" in the plan he had conceived at Biarritz.

As the tin operators argued Sir Philip's proposal, and

the meeting broke up into heated discussions, the key figure in the debate was the colorful Sir Cecil Clementi, G.C.M.C., K.C.M.G., Knight of Grace of the Order of St. John of Jerusalem, M.A., F.R.G.S., M.R.A.S., and Honorable Fellow of Magdalen College of Oxford. He was the song-writing, poetry-loving High Commissioner for Malaya, also Governor and Commander-in-Chief of the Straits Settlements.

Sir Cecil was happiest when he was writing such profound works as "Pervigilium Veneris," or composing his famous "Cantonese Love Songs," or penning his "Elements in Analysis of Thought," and "Summary of Geographical Observations Taken During a Journey from Kashgar to Kowloon."

But Sir Cecil was seldom able to indulge these esoteric pleasures. His constituents, the high- and low-cost groups, represented completely opposite interests, presenting constantly the same basic problem which now confronted the Association. Sir Cecil had to keep the peace between tall Howeson—the six-foot five-inch "upstart" of the Anglo-Oriental mining group which owned half a billion dollars' worth of tin properties and dredges in Nigeria, Malaya and Cornwall and were all high-cost producers—and F. E. Mair, who controlled thousands of pits in the Malayan Peninsula which produced tin in its cheapest and simplest form through alluvial operations.

The rivalry between these two elements flared anew at the Association's meeting, expressing the clash of interests which involved all parties concerned. Moving diplomatically between the opponents, Sir Cecil spoke soothingly to both parties and kept the meeting from falling apart.

It was Howeson, in the end, who got the plan adopted. He talked more than all the others combined, and every word he uttered had been approved in advance by Patiño, who said nothing at all. A commanding figure, Howeson asserted in his Oxford-accented speech: "Why, when we have so little tin and the mines are so short-lived, should we throw it to the world, to pile up in warehouses where it is unwanted? Let us mine conscientiously and stop extravagant losses and extravagant prices which will hit consumption later on."

Patiño and his son beamed at this. Vargas smiled. Half the Malayan delegation frowned.

Howeson asked for honest cooperation in the spirit as well as the letter of the proposals. At every opportunity he emphasized the need for honesty—honesty plus government supervision could not fail to bring about the desired results. There was no room, he asserted, for any group that would betray another to gain an advantage. This line of reasoning went a long way toward swinging the delegates.

But angry squabbles marked the discussions of what the actual quotas should be. The bitterness of the arguments is reflected in the report of the Tin Producers Association which covers the meeting:

> All the producing countries which participated in the original control plan were naturally anxious to obtain as favorable

a quota as possible when the details of the plan were under discussion; it was inevitable that some of the producers in almost every country, although agreeing with control in principle, felt that their government should have struck a better bargain.

Whether they could, or should, have been allotted a greater proportion of the world's limited tin production are questions upon which opinions are bound to differ. But the purposes of these notes is not to attempt to decide any contentious points, but to indicate how and why the quotas came to be as they are.

The original quotas allotted to the participants of the plan had to be gauged on some recognized basis, and the basis chosen, after much discussion and consideration, was the production total during 1929. The choice of some other year might have been more advantageous to certain participants. The Dutch, for example, would have preferred 1921, or an average of the intervening years, to be taken as a basis. This would have given them an advantage over all tin-producing countries, but would, incidentally, have been disastrous to Malaya. A year giving the greatest justice to all parties had to be chosen, if a mutual agreement were to be reached, and 1929 was selected, both because it was the last year of wholly unrestricted production, and also because it recorded the highest production ever attained.

Before Sir Philip's gavel signaled the end of the historic London meeting, a majority had agreed on an annual world production of 145,000 tons. Then the delegates raced to cable offices and telephone booths to notify their governments of the committee's action. The Netherlands ratified the agreement within forty-eight hours; Bolivia followed soon after. All the other countries represented put through the desired legislation with a minimum of delay, except the disgruntled Malay States, which did not make the necessary commitments for more than a year, and succeeded in dumping many thousands of tons of tin with no restrictions whatever on an already tin-sated world.

No outsider will ever know exactly how the conflicting tin interests were brought together. Industrialists have considered it ever since as one of the most skillfully executed pieces of cartel diplomacy ever handled, and those in the know give most of the credit to Patiño. Certainly it was his idea originally, and apparently the little man had much to do with the success of the convention. During the Association's meetings, which followed the initial session in Sir Philip's home, the lights burned until early morning in Patiño's hotel suite and many important tin men called on him long after most Londoners had retired.

The power of Patiño in the new cartel became obvious when the new list of its officers was announced, shortly after the convention's adjournment. The name at the top read: "His Excellency, Don Simon Patiño, President."

This honor pleased Patiño almost as much as Bolivia's new quota. The international quota itself had been so engineered that even now it was above the world consumption of 1930. Patiño dreamed of tin selling at $2,500 per ton, and dreaming further, he anticipated that perhaps the cartel arrangement might change the bears to bulls, with a consequent soaring of prices. In any event, the cartel was his pride and joy, and the teeth he had put in it would hurt only his competitors, never Patiño. Whatever happened, he would be benefited in the long run. He was one of the few men in the world with enough capital to hold out indefinitely. Finally, his cartel would show the politicians back home in Bolivia that he had done his best, and it would now become their responsibility to quiet the unrest of his starving workers.

This unrest had become an increasingly serious problem for Patiño during the four-year decline in tin values. Many of his workers had been laid off, and those who continued to work found their already pitiful incomes slashed even further. The voice of protest rose from the lowly, coca-drugged laborers, these despairing semi-slaves who had never even seen their fabulous absentee master, and who suffered with lung diseases and silicosis from the acid-charged air of the deep shafts. Some of the rebellious ones were silenced with bullets. Those who returned to work toiled grudgingly, deep in the illuminated nightmare corridors, drilling and blasting 15,000 feet above sea level.

Once Patiño had attempted to quiet the revolt by providing the workmen with a diet of Hollywood movies in a specially built Simon Patiño Theater on the company property at Llallagua. Visiting patrons were somewhat appalled by the contrast of the miserable, underfed, bewildered employees, their empty stomachs growling with the juices of narcotic leaves, blinking their eyes at the gold-plated luxuries displayed on the movie screen. The experiment only made matters worse.

Patiño could have raised wages out of his enormous surplus capital, but his books showed that he was losing $250 on every ton of tin ore his complaining natives produced in Bolivia, not to mention his losses in Pahang and Nigeria. He could have stopped his losses by closing down the mines, but such a step, even though only temporary, would have precipitated instant seizure of all his properties by the Bolivian government, or else it would have caused a revolution of such scope that the nation would have been plunged into a bloody civil war. Bolivia long since had learned to consider tin as a national heritage. No one, not even a man of Patiño's importance, dared tamper with the nation's greatest single source of income. Bolivia was already in default on payments to American holders of 25-year 8 per cent bonds issued in 1922, and Bolivian bondholders' committees had sprung up all over the United States. Bolivia's 7 per cents were also in default, and the United States Senate was investigating a statement that new loans of $23,000,000 had been "reluctantly" approved by the Bureau of Foreign and Domestic Commerce, even though Washington knew that the country had overborrowed.

Patiño did not even dare contemplate closing his mines, particularly at so critical a juncture in national affairs. Besides, he was a businessman, and it was always his first thought to handle any situation with as little cost as possible to Patiño, without regard for whatever it might cost anyone else.

Thus he had come to his Biarritz plan and helped engineer its adoption by the Association. He was now in a splendid position. Obviously he could not be expected to raise wages. Until speculation and new uses increased tin consumption, the world would have to absorb the surpluses and catch up with production. That might take years, of course. Patiño never lost sight of the fact that in the case of tin more factors than supply and demand controlled its behavior.

In selling his plan to the tin operators, however, Patiño had forgotten or else ignored the fact that everyone would not be gullible enough to believe that the new international agreements were firmly grounded in the honesty which Sir Philip had so carefully emphasized. The *Straits Times*, published in the Straits Settlements, particularly doubted the complete honesty of one of the participants. This paper, circulating throughout the Far East, made bold charges against Patiño's Bolivia. It said editorially: ". . . Meanwhile, with the Federated Malay States Government doing its best to hold down one of its staple industries . . . the Bolivians go on merrily turning out tin. Why should they worry? . . . Bolivia does not care who else restricts, she means to go ahead producing and the devil take the hindmost."

When the score was all added up, after the agreement had been reached by the tin operators, it was plain to the most astute observers that Patiño would continue to dominate the tin world through his enormous influence with the British government. This power had enabled him to accomplish his plan. The men gathered in Lygon Square had little choice, actually, but to follow a course which had already been set for them through previous secret conferences which Patiño and his agents had dominated. Patiño was the only man present at the convention who had nothing to lose by the success of the Patiño plan. This is best illustrated by the fact that Bolivia's tin quota was set at 24 per cent of world production, which the Pan American Union later declared was "actually too high to fill during some years."

In many ways, every tin man at the momentous meeting was simply a Patiño puppet, acting willingly or unwillingly, knowingly or in ignorance, on the little man's instructions. The tin king had lined up forces too powerful for anyone to resist.

But the organization he created did not find the life of cartelization an easy one. Obviously, it had frightening autocratic power. Its members, representing the governments of the tin-producing nations, had absolute authority to fix tin production quotas, and their respective governments had guaranteed to enforce those quotas.

The committee had a most cosmopolitan appearance when it met. There were the three extremely tall British representatives, sun-blackened veterans of colonial civil service. All the other members were little men: rotund Van Ketwich, representing the Netherlands; Phra Bahidda Nukara, a smart, almond-eyed Siamese prince; and correct, slim Antenor Patiño.

This committee of six met sometimes in the austere Colonial Office, in London, occasionally at the Palace of Peace in The Hague, oftener at Patiño's house in Paris. But wherever they met, they were confronted with the fact it was not enough to cut the production of tin.

Nor were their initial moves particularly happy ones. They began by setting the world quota of tin at 145,000 tons, but F. E. Mair, the Malayan low-cost producer, who had never been happy about the agreement in the first place, wrote a letter to the *Financial Times* in which he pointed out sarcastically that the quota was above 1930 consumption, and he added that consumption was still falling. The committee forthwith cut the quota to 125,000 tons. But two months later the world consumption picture was still gloomier, and the committee was forced, at a meeting in The Hague, to form a pool.

In this refinement of cartelization, the tin pool was an arrangement by which Sir John Campbell and Van Ketwich, committee members, acted for the Dutch government and a British syndicate whose membership was a secret. It was not difficult to identify at least one prominent member of this syndicate—Patiño. No one took seriously any denials of this speculation.

The function of the pool was to buy tin out of the growing surplus. Within two months they held 12,500 tons, and in another month they had jumped their holdings to 15,800 tons, or seven million dollars' worth. At this point, the committee helped the pool by cutting the world quota again, this time to 110,000 tons, which was about 55 per cent of 1929 production.

But the gap between production and consumption was not bridged. The pool spent three million dollars a month and bought up to 21,000 tons by 1932, at which point they were near the end of their rope.

The question in the minds of economists and financiers everywhere began to loom larger: Could the production of any world commodity be stabilized, relatively? Traditional economics, speaking from experience, said no. Less academic minds said yes. They pointed out that the tin industry was almost free from the control of banks, that 80 per cent of its controllers could already sit down around the table.

Worst of all, however, was the general sympathy and admiration that many observers felt for the tin cartel, the principal exceptions being those who were losing money as a result of it. There was a good deal of high-sounding talk about the cooperative element involved, and how it might one day rise above selfish interests.

It took another world war to demonstrate how the cartel system had wound its tentacles around the throats of free men everywhere, and how even a partially successful cartel could be a nail in democracy's coffin.

PARIS, Jan. 28 (UP).—The Duchesses of Windsor and Kent today wrested the title of world's best dressed woman away from Mme. Antenor Patiño, the "Tin Princess," whose husband is heir to one of the world's biggest fortunes, a poll of Parisian dressmakers showed.

The Duchesses, always near the top in fashion rankings, tied for first place in the United Press annual poll and the "Tin Princess" dropped back to third place.—New York Times, *January 29, 1940.*

14

The Princess of Tin

While Patiño was engaged in establishing his cartel, his son Antenor was occupied with the making of a most fortunate marriage. His lady was the Princess Cristina de Bourbon, daughter of the Duke and Duchess de Durcal, and niece of the King and Queen of Spain. She was black-eyed, exceedingly slim, graceful and gay. Fashion arbiters of Paris, London and Madrid were unanimous in agreeing that she "carried" her jewelry with greater perfection than any other woman in the world. It was an inspiring sight to see Cristina displaying diamonds, rubies, and combinations of emeralds and sapphires on her maidenly breast and graceful milk-white neck, and one could only admire the nonchalance with which she wore wide bracelets of magnificent jewels on her aristocratic arms.

Couturiers were in agreement, too, that no other European beauty had such exquisite taste in the matter of evening dresses. These Cristina selected from the smartest wardrobe possessed by any woman of the day. In sport clothes or décolletage, she was acknowledged as the best-dressed woman of her time, perhaps even in all history.

By any account Cristina was a dazzling princess. She ranked high in the Almanach de Gotha and she was qualified to reign as queen in any country. She never became a queen, but through the ironic circumstances of her marriage to the descendant of a lowly Bolivian Quechua, she acquired another title: Princess of Tin. Her romance with Antenor was possible only because the Spanish grandees of Madrid unaccountably failed to bar the Patiños socially.

Before Cristina met Antenor in Paris, Patiño's daughter Elena had already set her brother an example by marrying the Marquis del Merito, chamberlain to the King of Spain. This match was not as brilliant as Antenor's, because, of course, the poor Marquis was not a prince, but it was still of such importance in court circles that ruling monarchs were represented at the nuptials. Before the ceremony, both the Marquis and his fiancée had gifts of gold and baubles lavished upon them. Society gossips whispered that the bride's father had presented her husband with a check for $1,500,000 on the day before the wedding.

At a reception after the ceremony, held in the magnificent Patiño mansion on the Avenue Foch in Paris, new legends were born. One said that the check was displayed under a glass bell in the main salon, and powerful spotlights fixed on the ceiling were played on it through red and green filters so that everyone might be aware of Patiño's generosity. Patiño also gave the Marquis and his bride a battery of five Rolls-Royces, including town cars, sport and touring models.

The reception, however, did nothing to increase Patiño's popularity among the Bolivian colony in Europe, or with his countrymen back home in the Andes. Many invited Bolivians left in a rage when no one came forth to welcome them. Dozens of the Bolivians who had been especially invited wandered about the empty halls in search of the party before they stumbled upon it accidentally. A French butler who threw open the ballroom doors to these confused visitors revealed to them a scene of such brilliance that momentarily they forgot the affront and stared in fascination.

They saw a thousand guests thronging the spacious, vaulted chamber—men and women representing the socially élite of every European capital. Great Britain's royalty was present. A Greek princess danced with the son of Rumania's king. Italy's titled families drank champagne d'Honneur with Patiño himself. The aristocracy of France, members of the Hohenzollern family, and scions of Belgium's royal lines waltzed to the music of four orchestras which were banked amid floral settings around the immense walls.

But no one came forward to welcome the Bolivians. No one offered Patiño's countrymen a glass of wine so that they could toast the bride. They were received only by a corps of detectives, who ushered them into a salon where they might admire the wedding gifts.

The gifts were distinguished particularly by three million dollars' worth of jewels, which were piled on great mahogany tables in dime-store arrangements and with about as much indifference. The Bolivians saw gift cards signed by the wealthiest men in the world, from the Morgans of America to the Zaharoffs of the Balkans. Dictator Gomez, of Venezuela, who had amassed a fortune of $100,000,000 by graft alone, had sent gifts to the daughter of the only South American whose fortune topped his own. Maharajas of India, railroad tycoons and leaders of every stripe had sent expressions of their friendship and esteem, mostly silver and gold, diamonds, rubies and pearls from scores of nations.

Amid all this magnificence the Bolivians stood alone. No member of the Patiño family said a word to them. Still bewildered by such a reception, one Bolivian asked a detective, "Has there not been some mistake?"

"No, Monsieur," the detective assured him, "there has been no mistake. What mistake could there be?"

The Bolivians slipped out of the great house quietly, into the foggy Parisian night. It was then that some of them remembered Patiño's struggle to get into the Club Social, and the truth dawned on them. The slight had been the little man's revenge.

Mestizos like Patiño, who heard the story of the Paris snubbing much later in Bolivia, professed to be amused by it, but among the Spanish grandees and in high political circles there was stirred up a resentment that lasted for years. It was as though a king had spat upon his own flag.

Nonetheless Patiño moved from one triumph to another when his daughter's wedding was followed by the marriage of Antenor and Cristina in Madrid on April 8, 1931. Patiño gave the bride five million dollars' worth of diamonds, and an amount of cash that was never disclosed. To his son, the aging father presented a check for $10,000,000, thus bringing Antenor's already huge fortune to a reputed billion.

The Patiños journeyed *en famille* to Madrid for the ceremony. The only absent member of the family was Rene, the second son, who had gone to a sanitarium after a tragic experience at the Hotel Plaza in New York a few years before. The Patiños never spoke of this sad affair.

They spoke often, however, about another tragedy—the continued fall of tin. Even as he rode beside the King of Spain to the wedding, Patiño could not keep his mind from this fact. His cartel was not yet working properly. Patiño stared unseeingly at the faces of Madrid citizens who stood cheering along the bridal procession's route. He could think only of the cable he had received a few hours earlier. London had advised him that tin was down to $485 a ton.

Patiño survived the wedding ceremony, but he was in a state of anxiety and his relief was obvious when the Archbishop pronounced, "*Benedicamus Domino.*" Albina thought it a good moment to pass him another cable which she had been sparing him. It was from his general manager, Arturo Loaiza, and it read: "Catavi workers demonstrating."

When Patiño and Albina returned to their suite in Madrid's royal palace, they were greeted by a perturbed secretary who gave his employer a third cable.

"It is not good news," the secretary warned gravely.

Patiño let the cable drop to the floor.

"Tell me," he said. "I do not wish to read it."

The secretary's voice showed his deep anxiety.

"Tin closed in London today at $470, Mr. Patiño."

That night, in direct violation of his doctor's orders, Patiño smoked seven two-dollar cigars, one more than his allowance, and he overdrank his quota of champagne.

A physician who had examined the tin king in Paris only the year before had cross-examined his patient on the subject of his vices, and Patiño had cheated himself by lying about his regular schedule of six cigars a day and a pint of champagne every night. He outwitted the doctor neatly and foolishly.

"How many cigars do you smoke, Monsieur?" the specialist inquired.

"Twelve," Patiño told him.

"Well, you must cut down to six. And champagne?"

"I drink a quart a day."

"From now on, only a pint."

On the night of his son's wedding, the little man felt a definite need for a seventh cigar and a second pint of champagne as he struggled to work out a plan that would save his tin empire. It was plain that his cartel's teeth had not bitten as deeply into the problem as he had anticipated. Quota reductions had not been enough. The sentimental traders had not behaved this time in the way he expected. Men who had tin to sell still sold it to those who wanted to buy. The selling was indiscriminate, as it had been before cartelization. Old, surplus tin was offered in world markets along with newly mined tin, and there was too much of both. Manufacturers who needed tin got it on the old basis of supply and demand. That, Patiño decided, was the root of the evil, and inspiration came to him. To save tin, it was necessary to eliminate supply and demand.

Calling Albina, he told her his idea: "Tin producers must also be tin buyers!" Then he outlined his scheme to her carefully and they worked out together the fine points of an enormous undertaking. Early next morning, before Antenor and his bride departed on their honeymoon trip to the scented gardens of the Château de Valrose, Patiño stepped aboard his private plane and flew to London.

As the world's foremost authority on monopoly, Patiño was now in his element as he planned the most comprehensive cartel restriction ever attempted in history. Six months later, with the concurrence of the Tin Association's members and their governments, the gigantic "tin pool" was born. Patiño and a small group of conspirators put through the resolutions in record time.

This time the plan was foolproof. When it was announced in September, 1931, the scheme had been in operation for several weeks. Tin men were now tin buyers. Backed by a cash pool of enormous size, the ITC took its first step by "segregating" much of the visible supply of tin from Malaya to Bolivia. As producers offered tin, ITC bought tin. The price-determining principles of supply and demand vanished overnight. Tin began to climb. Six months after Patiño returned to Paris from his long conferences in London, the metal was being quoted on the exchange at $705 per ton, and in another three months the price had reached $1,000 per ton.

On the floor of the United States Congress, Senators and Representatives attacked the "evil monopoly" vigorously. Representative S. D. McReynolds (Dem., Tenn.), chairman of the House Foreign Affairs Committee, asserted: "It appears that substantially complete control of the tin production of the world is now lodged in the International Tin Committee, which is composed of, or participated in, by representatives of the governments of tin-producing countries, namely, the United Kingdom, British Malaya, Nigeria, the Dutch East Indies, Siam, Bolivia, French Indo-China and Portugal.

". . . It appears that since this scheme was put into effect, the price of tin in New York has risen from twenty-two cents per pound to fifty-two cents per pound and there is no evidence before this committee to indicate that the price may not be raised indefinitely."

A note of particular annoyance crept into McReynolds' voice when he called attention to the fact that the United States, although it consumed more than half of the monopoly's product, did not have "a single tin smelter of its own."

Another Congressman, Millard F. Caldwell (Dem., Florida), deplored the fact that tin prices had risen materially because the tin needed for automobiles, canning and a thousand other requirements had to be shipped to America "around two sides of a world triangle."

To all this uproar from Yankee Congressmen, Patiño paid not the slightest attention. They had roared before and nothing ever came of it. Patiño was in an excellent mood. He smoked his cigars, drank his champagne, and sat in his library turning the gadgets that animated his $50,000 model of the Llallagua mine. He pushed a button and the elevators ran to the different levels. He pushed another button and ore cars skidded around the curves of Cuadro San Miguel, and climbed to Cuadro Victoria II. The miniature cars even passed a model of the underground chapel which the pious Bolivian miners had built 3,000 feet in the poisonous bowels of the earth.

As he looked at this chapel, Patiño felt an emotion that was as close as he could come to pity. What if his workmen were smoldering for revolt? They were a pretty good lot, after all. Impulsively, Patiño rang for his secretary and dictated a cable to his general manager. It read:

"Arturo, open up my main mansion in Cochabamba. There is to be a great day. Invite all my workmen to enter into my palace. I wish them to see the glory of it all, its architecture, its art treasures, its tapestries, its marble and golden decorations, its fountains and its fixtures, its great French beds, its American plumbing, its kitchens and its cellars, and its masterpieces upon the walls."

For Patiño, this was a sentimental moment. He felt that he had made a great benefaction. He was a good employer who had good workmen in the best of all possible tin monopolies.

PARIS, June 2—Simon I. Patiño, the Bolivian, who is believed to be one of the world's ten richest men, passed his seventieth birthday today wrapped in the mysterious seclusion that has led Paris to call him the "tin hermit."

Outside his palace on the Avenue Foch, Bolivian guards patrolled the sidewalk. Inside, surrounded by a battery of secretaries, he spent the morning reading the latest news from the Chaco. His associates say he aids in guiding his country's war finances. Señor Patiño is the Bolivian Minister to France, but he never goes to diplomatic functions and seldom visits the embassy.—New York Times, *June 3, 1935.*

15

The Voice of Despair

IF THE thought of opening his Cochabamba palace to his serfs made Patiño feel like a beneficent employer, it was one of the few opportunities he ever had to consider himself in this light. His labor relations were anything but happy most of the time.

This inability to get along with workmen, generated by Patiño's natural instinct to exploit a man rather than employ him, usually resulted in tragic, bitter conflict, but once or twice it bordered on the ludicrous. The Riviera chuckled over one of these infrequent incidents when Patiño clashed with the gardeners who made his vast acreage of roses and hedges and private forests of imported trees and shrubs an eighth wonder of the Continent.

These Italian and French workmen grumbled at their low wages as they labored in the shadow of a palace so magnificent that it stood out even in a resort world famous for lavishness. They asked for a small raise. Patiño not only refused, he discharged them all on the spot.

"That will fix you," he told their leader. "Get off my estate!"

The gardeners refused to obey this order. Instead they picketed the palace. Those who were not walking in the picket line sat on the lawns and ate lunches which their wives brought to them, and slept at night rolled up in blankets beneath the hedges, which were now growing scraggly. When it rained, they found refuge under the splendid imported trees. Amused fellow residents called Patiño's trouble a lay-down strike. Finally Patiño called the police, and the gendarmes ended the strike by ejecting the strikers.

But shortly before Patiño conceived the generous thought of permitting his Cochabamba workers to stare at the luxury their labor had created, he had a far more serious labor struggle on his hands, one that became an international scandal. There had been strikes in the mine fields before, in which scores of workers were shot by army and police officials. The one in question, however, surpassed all the others in violence.

It came about over a demand for higher wages, which was the constant complaint of Patiño's underpaid employees. The tin king had previously authorized increases as high as 50 per cent, a magnanimous concession on the face of it, but one which failed to take into account Bolivia's inflationary conditions. With living costs increased as much as 1,000 per cent, the miners wound up, even after increases, with incomes no higher than forty to fifty cents per day. This time they asked for more money and a Christmas bonus of a month's pay. Both demands were refused.

One night a howling rose from the heights of Catavi. It was the howling of desperate, maddened men—ragged, diseased, oppressed human moles. From rotting lungs, from throats eaten raw by the poison of the mines, they shrieked their despair and anger. With imploring hands raised high, they besought the thunder god to join with them against their oppressor, and in the strange pattern of their religion, they prayed simultaneously to the Virgin Mary.

The protest began as a wild, purposeless chorus from the lips of miners, their wives and their babies alike, screaming in the Quechua dialect. It had a crashing power that impressed as much as it frightened the callous white bosses who heard this voice of despair. It was not wholly despair, they realized as they listened. As the tide of sound welled higher, the tempo changed as the Quechuas became conscious for the first time that they had actually dared to make a protest at all. They had endured in silence, now they were doing a thing heretofore unthinkable. They exulted in the discovery, tasting a sweet freedom, reveling in a hope never before known to them.

Delirious giggling replaced the screeching as understanding dawned. It was a strange thing, and far more frightening to the white bosses, to hear the Quechuas laugh. So rare is the Indian's laughter that some of the bosses had never heard the phenomenon. They were laughing now, an abandoned, terrible sound rolling in a weird community of discords from the heights of Catavi.

Brilliant searchlights from Patiño's hydro-electric plant played over the unarmed mob, disclosing the gaunt, bow-legged, squat men, their bronze parchment skin stretched tightly over high cheekbones, roaring with wild laughter. The searchlight only increased their unholy mirth, because it was a new reminder of their master's misplaced beneficence. They wanted money for food and shelter and their simple necessities. Patiño gave them electric light bulbs, a 5,700-foot golf course, a hot-water swimming pool and American movies. Thus they only howled the louder when Patiño's searchlight swept them.

Soldiers quartered near by heard the commotion, and an excited officer told them that it was a treasonous uprising. Forming quickly, they marched up Catavi's heights—and wavered before the unearthly power of the unarmed demonstrators. The quality of that blind appeal, rolling down in waves of passionate, unintelligible sound, was something the soldiers could understand. They knew what poverty meant, and they had suffered privation and hunger, consequently they sympathized in secret with the demonstrators. But Patiño's taxes paid their wages, those taxes that were 90 per cent of Bolivia's income. Remembering that, the soldiers raised their guns and fired when the order came.

Machine-gun bullets slugged the bodies of the startled

workers. Men and women fell dead, their babies in their arms. A frightful groan welled up from the wounded, mingled with a mass sigh of utter despair which rose spontaneously from the lips of those who had escaped the bullets. The miners fell back, carrying their wounded, as the soldiers poured death again and again into their disorderly, retreating ranks. More workers pitched into the silica dust, now churned into clouds beneath the frantic feet of the living who sought escape into the eerie gray smoke-screen. But the inexorable searchlights from the hydro-electric plant picked out new targets and the slaughter went on.

Next day the Indian President, Enrique Penaranda del Castillo, declared a state of siege. Mauricio Hochschild, Patiño's rival tin baron, expressed an official alarm. Carlos Aramayo, still another payer of low wages, appeared to be full of forebodings. As for the Indians, they spent the time in sorrowfully counting their casualties: 400 dead, 600 wounded. Penaranda dismissed these figures as nonsense. Only nineteen were killed and a score or so injured, he said.

No amount of official pooh-poohing and soft-pedaling could still the echo of that awful protest and its tragic consequences. The President's nine-man cabinet resigned. A wave of angry revolt swept all Bolivia, and in the dawn before Christmas Day, men emerged on the streets of La Paz with machine guns and fought for four hours up and down the cobbled thoroughfares of the capital. Penaranda fled to Chile, Aramayo immured himself in the Spanish Embassy. Hochschild was jailed. A new *caudillo* was sworn into office. Bolivia had a new master, but Patiño's title to his five million acres of tin was unaffected, and so he was still master of both.

The massacre resulted in several investigations, one of which was conducted by a scholarly group of Americans. They found the Bolivians 75 per cent illiterate, and their school system a joke. Everything bad in Bolivia, they concluded, was caused by centuries of poverty and ignorance and they returned a severe indictment against the exploiters for their greed. It was a challenge to the Americas to raise the standards of the country, they declared.

"Bolivian law," said the report, "requires that mining enterprises and haciendas maintain primary schools for their employees." But the joker in this fine-sounding legislation was that all decisions as to teachers and the selection of subjects taught lay in the hands of the owners.

Concerning the labor situation, the report said: "The Commission was impressed wherever it went with the total absence of free association of the workers and collective bargaining. The legal minimum wage rates are clearly insufficient to maintain a decent and healthy standard of living. There does not exist in Bolivia a single safe water system under proper control. The diet of the average Bolivian worker falls far below the standards considered necessary for good health."

The Commission went on to criticize all other sanitary

conditions, and deplored the lack of proper medical and hospital care.

In fairness, it must be noted that Patiño had made efforts to alleviate some of these conditions. He had schools on his mining properties which were attended by 1,470 pupils, and he had a hospital for his miners staffed by six doctors, eight nurses and three pharmacists. But this was scarcely a dent in the country's total situation, and it did nothing to remedy the basic problem: the extreme poverty of the workers. Patiño's great wealth could have transformed Bolivia.

In summing up, the American Commission—made up of impartial lawyers, judges and unionists—spoke a fundamental truth: "The recognition and fostering of the self-respect and dignity of the individual lies at the foundation of a labor economy in a democracy. Our aim must be the achievement of a standard of living compatible with that dignity. No nation has as yet fully achieved that objective. The Commission cannot forbear the hope that its report will make some modest contribution to the material and moral progress of the conditions of labor in Bolivia."

Notwithstanding these circumstances, the result obtained by Patiño Mines during 1929 should be considered satisfactory. We have been able to obtain this result by reason of greater efficiency in the technical and administrative services, as a consequence of the program of expansion approved and authorized by the board of directors in 1927. . . .

Patiño Mines has faced the tin crisis in 1929 by employing more efficient working systems, rather than by resorting to other means, such as reduction of salaries and wages, etc., a policy which it will maintain invariably so long as permitted by market conditions and by tax laws now in force in Bolivia, where the mining properties of the company are located.—From the annual report of Patiño Mines and Enterprises Consolidated, *1929.*

16

Benevolent Host

WITH THE memory of the Catavi massacre still fresh in their minds, the police and military of Cochabamba were justifiably apprehensive early one morning in the fall of 1933 when Indians in great numbers began pouring into the city. They came in bronze waves, a phenomenal influx such as not even the oldest member of the constabulary could remember. The number of Quechuas appearing would have been remarkable for a festival day.

One of the youngest policemen, whose station was on the outskirts of town, became uneasy after he had counted hundreds descending from the heights. The barefooted men and women, poncho covered, sucking their cuds of coca, passed him in quiet and melancholy groups of twos and dozens. Some carried babies, others held the hands of older children who trotted beside them.

The influx began at daybreak. By 7 A.M., the young

officer estimated that 2,000 Indians had trudged past his post en route to the main plaza of the municipality. If he had been more experienced, the patrolman would have concluded much earlier that the mass descent meant trouble, but he did not become alarmed enough to report the situation until nearly 4,000 Indians had streamed into the plaza. Other patrolmen were even more delinquent, either asleep at their posts or enjoying the company of *chola* mistresses.

When the errant patrolmen finally awoke to what was happening, they reported in panic to headquarters, where they found things in a bedlam. The sergeant in charge, shocked and frightened out of his wits, anticipating a counter-massacre, had already notified the military garrison, urging them to march quickly against the invaders. Meanwhile, the police were being formed into heavily armed squads, some equipped with antique tear-gas bombs, to proceed into the battle.

Only a few minutes later, the officers of both police and army had to retire and hide their embarrassment when they learned that the Quechuas had no more violent intention than to inspect Don Simon Patiño's palace. The tin king's wholly unexpected beneficence, coming so closely on the heels of the bloody Catavi struggle, had totally confounded the forces of order. Only the Indians appeared not to see the irony of the situation.

The doors of the great palace were thrown open at noon, after the workers had stood shivering two abreast in long lines for hours before the unlived-in residence of their absentee master. In this interval, they were permitted to admire the exterior of the lofty structure, thrusting its strange peaks and towers of marble and granite higher than cathedral spires into Cochabamba's thin air. This favorite dwelling of Patiño's, in which he never dwelt, was the work of scores of imported talents —Italian artisans, British gardeners, French interior decorators and American plumbers.

While this army of imported specialists was building the architectural monstrosity, the starving Quechuas viewed the spectacle with bewilderment from the doorways of their squat adobe huts. They could not understand this palace, nor the magnificent mausoleum which Patiño was building simultaneously a few kilometers away with marble imported from the quarries of Belgium and Italy, and transported in dozens of flat cars across the Andes from Buenos Aires and from Antofagasta.

The Quechuas could not know, of course, that the palace and mausoleum were the result of Patiño's "king complex," and that they were modeled (rather remotely) after King Philip II's famous Escorial, twenty-seven miles northwest of Madrid. To blot out the memory of stinking adobe huts and shallow rock-covered graves, all of which were part of the *mestizo* past he wanted to forget, Patiño desired, both in life and in death, a splendor such as South America had never seen. Huts and shallow graves were good enough for the neighbors he had left behind.

Splendor he wanted and splendor he got, in fantastic

quantity and quality. After they had built the main palace, Patiño's imported geniuses proceeded to construct two of the strangest and most expensive buildings ever to distort a landscape. These secondary structures were dismissed as "dependencies," but they cost more than $20,000,000 to build and furnish.

When the entire estate was completed, it resembled nothing else on earth. The Spanish artists, Greek tile workers, Irish lacemakers, Dutch sculptors and Syrian rug men had added the final touches, to say nothing of the copper pipe from Indiana and the fur-covered, plastic-trimmed toilets installed by the American plumbers beside blue marble bathtubs as large as swimming pools. In this international potpourri, lighting systems designed in Schenectady provided illumination for fixtures used by Mme. de Pompadour, which were wired by electricians from Hollywood.

Patiño's fabulous wealth and his love of pomp and glitter were reflected everywhere in the finished product. There were such items as gold doorknobs, tin walls, copper walls, and walls covered with embroidered velvet on which the master's initials were blazoned in big gold letters. From the museums of a dozen world capitals, and from private collections as well, had come five hundred crates full of paintings to hang over heroic sculptured mantelpieces, and in the vaulted halls and galleries. Five hundred square yards of sun rooms, with decorative tile floors laid by artisans from Wales, presented to the beholder ancient Chinese prints and tapestries valued at more than a million dollars.

It was this Arabian Nights lushness which the momentarily benevolent Patiño now wished his workmen to see. Only a psychiatrist would be qualified to say exactly what prompted this impulse. To the ordinary observer, it seemed like a rich child showing off his Shetland pony to a street urchin in a wobbly cheesebox cart, a billionaire in a Rolls-Royce passing a peasant on a jackass. In more American terms, it was Little Orphan Annie being snooted by the banker's daughter.

Some Cochabambites, however, saw a more practical motive in Patiño's gesture. Knowing Patiño so well, they theorized that the sight of these dazzling earthly goods was expected to impress the simple Quechuas so much that they would never again dare to cross the man who was able to amass such riches. Only a mind like Patiño's would be likely to imagine that Gobelins and Lyons velvet brocades would change the miners' thinking and make them less susceptible to labor organizations, and more amenable to the foremen who drove them on to still greater efforts in the unhealthy shafts.

If this was actually Patiño's idea, the results must have been one of the major shocks in his life.

When the doors were opened that momentous day, Patiño's general manager, Arturo Loaiza, beamed upon the multitude of emaciated workers who stood sucking their coca quids. Promptly at noon, Loaiza looked at his watch, swung his arm in a signal, the mammoth bronze doors were swung open by French butlers dressed in evening clothes, and the line started marching slowly forward.

Velvet ropes had been stretched on brass standards everywhere in the house to keep the visitors safely at a distance from the treasures on the walls, to prevent their dirty hands from coming into contact with the furnishings. It was bad enough, so the staff thought, to have bare feet tracking the marble floors and soiling the carpets and rugs.

The Indians marched through the doors and began to sift through the palace. Some were guided through rear entrances to see the swimming pools and the scented gardens filled with rare flowers from Japan, mimosa from Nice, wild honeysuckle from Georgia swamps and hedges from old English lanes. They saw hothouses filled with white orchids, aviaries inhabited by birds from every land, their cages controlled by thermostat to the temperature of their native habitat.

These were strange sights for the simple Indians, and some of them were frightened. Babies cried and their mothers moaned and called upon Chiroquella, the thunder god. Some thought they were in heaven, but others considered themselves in hell. Nearly all were dazed and confused.

Loaiza and his helpers were busy keeping the lines moving in the front and out at the rear, pointing to this and motioning to that, never forgetting to remind the visitors how fortunate they were and how good was their master.

As he supervised the proceedings, Loaiza told himself that the affair was going well, but this delusion was the result of his concentration upon the treasures under his care. He could see only that the wine was still intact in the cellar, that the vaults of jewels were undisturbed in the library, and the silver and gold plate in the butler's pantry was safe.

Loaiza did not know that resentment had made its ugly appearance until an aide brought him the news, just as he was impressing an Indian in a ragged poncho with the miracle of water produced by turning a silver faucet over a lavatory off the master's room. Interrupted by his worried assistant, Loaiza ran to the center of the disturbance in the main salon.

Dozens of Indians and half-breeds were shouting at the top of their lungs. They were calling Patiño names, of which "*bastado*" was the most frequently used. There were other names even more emphatic which cannot be translated accurately. A dozen of the shouting men held bright crayons in their hands, crayons of all colors. Some crayon holders were not shouting, but were hard at work covering priceless antique Chinese tapestries and French velvet with pornographic cartoons. One of the industrious despoilers knew how to write, and he was laboriously scribbling insulting things under the name Patiño. Some of the artists stood upon the backs of their comrades so that they could inscribe dirty words in higher places.

Loaizo was stunned and horrified. The ungrateful visitors, guilty and innocent alike, were herded unceremoniously out of the palace, routed from the gardens, the lawns, the basements, the cellars and the bedrooms of the estate. This exodus took a long time, and it took many foremen, clerical workers and trusted servants to do the job.

When the last squawling infant had been dragged through the main gate by its mother, and the final unwashed miner sent on his way by a firm hand at his back, the bronze doors of the palace were banged shut. They have remained shut ever since.

Patiño's experiment in benevolence, like all his other ventures in human relations, was a flat failure.

"Those of us who have toiled for liberty in South America have but plowed the sea."—Simon Bolivar.

Several days ago a plainly dressed, undistinguished-looking man walked through the Waldorf-Astoria lobby and asked the desk clerk about rooms.

He then proceeded to sign the name "Patiño" with a flourish and order the best suite available. They gave him a sumptuous apartment overlooking Park Avenue.

Patiño, Bolivia's greatest tin king and one of the big financial figures of the world, has temporarily wearied of his magnificent home in Paris and hence pays the United States a visit. He is also negotiating a business deal. . . .—New York Times, *December 5, 1933.*

17

Cartel Cabal

THE HISTORY of tin, and consequently of Patiño, from the creation of tin control until the second World War, is illuminated by numerous official reports, and the rather frank commentaries of financial publications. Pieced together, they provide a general picture of how the tin cartel worked until war upset its applecart again.

It must be emphasized that the control introduced by the Tin Producers' Association was never looked upon as a sinister plot, as in the cartel arrangements by which German firms are alleged to have gained virtual control of American drug and chemical industries. Financiers regarded tin control admiringly as a shrewd move to save a world industry from disaster. But in effect, this control actually put the world's governments at the mercy of a few men in the acquisition and use of a vital commodity. In particular, it placed Patiño in an enviable position, which the United States discovered to its embarrassment when the tin crisis came.

Five years after tin control was introduced, the Association published a booklet titled "Facts About Tin Control," which celebrated the virtues of the cartel. Under the head of general benefits, the pamphlet asserted that tin control in four years had:

"1. Reduced the stocks of tin from the abnormal level of 60,547 tons, reached in April, 1932, to a more normal level of 20,000 tons.

"2. Correlated production with consumers' demands, so ensuring that, while ample supplies are available to meet any sudden increase in consumption, unwanted tin is left unmined.

"3. Raised the price of tin from the uneconomic level of 100 pounds a ton to its present level of approximately 225 pounds, which affords the producers as a whole a reasonable profit, despite the limitation of output.

"4. Stabilized the price of tin at this reasonable level for nearly two years, a stabilization that has not only benefited the consumer—in eliminating the risk of carrying large stocks, which otherwise might be liable to heavy and sudden depreciation, and enabling costs to be planned well ahead—but has also given all tin-mining companies a chance to re-establish themselves financially, and to pay dividends to shareholders.

"5. Established a research organization which, while giving a service to consumers, is also designed to protect and develop existing tin markets, and to discover new ones.

"6. Lengthened the life of the mines by conserving for future production that part of their tin ore resources which is unwanted today."

To bolster its argument, the Association then quoted the report of the Sub-Commission on Tin of the World Economic Conference, dated July 27, 1933. The quotations were highly complimentary.

Under the heading "Mechanism of Tin Control," the Association next undertook to answer some of its critics. It dealt first with the most frequent charge, the complaint by individual tin-producing countries that their governments had made bad bargains when the quotas were being set, a question upon which, the report noted, "opinions are bound to differ." The basis of these complaints was the setting of the year 1929 as a basis for allotting the quotas. This had, as was pointed out earlier, upset the Dutch, who would have preferred 1921 or any year immediately thereafter because their high production would have given them an advantage over every other producing country, particularly Malaya. The Association chose 1929, it declared, "both because it was the last year of wholly unrestricted production, and also because it recorded the highest production ever attained."

Inevitably, of course, the choice of that year and the subsequent allocation of quotas hurt some producers, notably low-cost producers in Malaya and elsewhere. The Malayan government came under fire for consenting so readily to the tin control agreement. Taking note of this criticism, the Association's pamphlet made an accurate analysis of Malaya's position in relation to Bolivia and the Dutch East Indies, as follows:

"Those who are disposed to criticize the Malayan Government for agreeing to certain details of this agreement seem to have forgotten the crisis with which Malaya herself was faced. The tin and rubber industries are the most important means of livelihood in that country; upon them depends the bulk of the revenue. Both were in great distress; and this, apart from depleting revenue beyond the danger point, created social problems that called for immediate action. A decision which would save the tin industry became a *national* necessity as well as being essential to the greater number of tin producers. It so happened that Bolivia and the Dutch East Indies were faced with the same problem, in that their revenue and national welfare depended largely upon the prosperity of the tin industry. Had it not been for this fact, many authorities hold that Malaya would not have been successful in making as good a bargain as she did.

"It should be added that an agreement was more urgently required by Malaya than by the Dutch East Indies, since the Dutch mines are government controlled, while the Malayan mines are owned by a multiplicity of individuals and companies, and shareholders demand an explanation for lack of dividends."

The original signers of the agreement were not only critical of each other, but they were even more unhappy when later participants in the control were given quotas which seemed overgenerous. This argument was never wholly resolved, but the Association contended in its book of "Facts" that three factors had been considered in setting these later quotas: the effect of the potential production of these countries on the International Control Plan; the inevitable growth of these countries' production if it were left uncontrolled; the maintaining of existing standards, which would be impossible if the countries were not permitted to participate.

Summing up this important point, the Association declared frankly: "It is now agreed by all but a very small minority, that the tin producers who were already in the scheme have gained more—by these concessions that were made—in the stability of prices and conditions that have been maintained, than they would have lost by a further big growth in uncontrolled production, which in all probability would have brought a return of the conditions that existed before control was introduced. Production control is vital to the tin industry until the industrial demand for tin reaches a figure approximating the previous levels: and the price paid for its efficient continuance was not high so far as these later quotas was concerned."

The report next unfolded, briefly, the scheme by which the International Tin Committee in 1934 began to untie itself from its self-imposed restrictions. By that time the world situation had begun to improve, and the Association found itself specifically prevented by its agreement from changing its quota allocations frequently to keep up with new industrial demands for tin. There was a danger that this situation would endanger the whole price structure of tin and cause the wide fluctuations in the market which had characterized the days before control. A sudden increase in demand, which the producers might not be able to fill for some time, would create a time lag handmade for the speculator, who would be able to push up the price and make a quick killing.

To avoid this possibility, the International Tin Committee devised a buffer stock scheme. The idea was to acquire 8,282 tons of additional tin, which would be held in reserve, under the control of the Committee and administered by a sub-committee representing the four original signatory countries. This acquisition was made possible by creating an additional quota for the four, "in proportion to their standard tonnage."

Patiño and his friends made sure that the buffer stock scheme would benefit no one but themselves. It was made plain that the stock belonged absolutely to the individual producers who supplied it, and any profits resulting from its sale would go to them. The advantage of the buffer stock plan were set forth most appealingly in the Committee's report:

"Apart from affording producers an opportunity to mine more tin, the Buffer Stock Plan acts as a safeguard to consumers, in that supplies of tin suddenly and urgently required are obtainable from this source at a reasonable price; while the Committee, by virtue of its powers to re-purchase the tin with the proceeds of sales, will be instrumental in preventing any wide variations in price, such as were known in pre-control days."

A particularly sore point in the minds of tin consumers in 1934 was the differential between the cost of producing tin and the stabilized price for it which the Association had set. The more bitter critics called it outright robbery, and even the milder ones said it was unreasonable. As for the producers, Patiño and some of the other top operators thought the differential was not great enough.

"Facts About Tin Control" went no further than to say that the present margin was "generally reasonable," and it attempted a discussion of the costs and the price of tin which is worth reading in part:

"Tin mining companies, it must be remembered, do not produce metallic tin, as bought by the consumer at the price published in the press, but a concentrate containing from 60 per cent to 75 per cent of metal. The assay of a high-grade ore may yield about 72 per cent of metal. This means that, if the price of tin is 230 pounds a ton, the gross return to the producer is about 165 pounds a ton of concentrates at 72 per cent of metal.

"Out of this gross yield, the producer has to provide for the mining costs, the government royalty of export tax, the cost of transport to the smelter, the smelting cost, the marketing charges, overhead expenses, depreciation of plant and amortization of capital, as well as dividends for the shareholders.

"After allowing for royalty, freight, smelting and marketing charges, the average net yield for high-grade concentrates is about 138 pounds a ton, when the price of the metal is about 230 pounds a ton. The actual mining cost, as already stated, is a very variable factor, not only in different countries, but even in regard to different properties within the same producing country.

"In Malaya, for example, the mining cost varies from below 30 pounds a ton of concentrates in the case of two or three very fortunately placed companies, to over 100 pounds a ton in the case of the higher-cost producers. It may be assumed that the average mining cost for the low-cost producers, who do not represent any very large proportion of the total, is certainly not below 38 pounds a ton. With the metal at 230 pounds a ton such producers would accordingly retain 100 pounds a ton of concentrates, out of which to provide for overhead expenses, depreciation of plant, amortization of capital and dividends for the shareholders.

"But in the case of the producers whose mining cost is in the neighborhood of 100 pounds a ton of concentrates, only 38 pounds would remain to cover these four items; and it is doubtful whether there would be sufficient to allow for the payment of any dividend if adequate provision is made for the depletion of their asset.

"There remain the many thousands of fossickers [1] and hand workers who are scattered over all the tinfields in the world—such as the dulang washers in British Malaya, and the tributors in Nigeria, Siam and elsewhere. These

[1] Fossicker—a miner who searches scattered or abandoned workings.

individual miners depend upon tin for their livelihood."

Against this professionally gloomy picture of tin operations, enough to bring tears to the eyes of a stockholder, could be balanced the statement issued the year before, covering the income of Patiño Mines & Enterprises, Consolidated, during the second half of 1933. After depreciation and extraordinary taxes, and including other income, the Patiño take was estimated at 300,000 pounds, at the annual rate of .434 pound a share on the 1,380,316 shares outstanding. At an exchange rate of $4.50, this amounted to $1.95 a share annually, after depreciation and taxes. Even in the bad year of 1932, Patiño Mines had shown an operating profit of approximately 169,000 pounds after depreciation and taxes; and in 1931, probably the worst year of all in the history of tin, Patiño Mines returned an operating profit of more than 300,000 pounds after taxes and depreciation, even though the price of tin was then the lowest since 1898.

Yet the Association could paint a blandly forbidding picture of tin operations, and then in its statement of "facts" could go on to argue that the tin consumer was not so directly concerned with the price of tin as long as it was "reasonable and stable." In support of this argument, the Association's pamphlet quoted from a speech made in Commons by Sir Arthur Michael Samuel, M.P., whom it described parenthetically as "also an important manufacturer." Sir Arthur declaimed:

"When manufacturers do not know what prices of

their raw materials are from day to day, it throws their business out of gear. . . . When there is no stability in the price of raw material, whether brought about by gambling or not, our manufacturers dare not extend. They do not know whether they will make or lose by the wide variations in prices and they hold back. The first man to suffer is the workingman."

There was no doubt that tin control had stabilized prices. In 1920, to take an extreme year, tin had reached a high of 419½ pounds and descended to a low of 195 pounds. When control began to be effective, it was able to prevent the variation from average from amounting to no more than 10 per cent, over a period of twenty-two months.

The effectiveness of control was further underlined by the Association's blunt statement that production outside the plan had never been more than 15 per cent of the world's production.

In spite of the Association's ardent defense of itself in "Facts About Tin Control," there were by 1935, the year of its publication, cries in both the English Parliament and the United States for an investigation of the International Tin Pool. Writing in *Commerce and Finance*, Jules Backman, vice-president of Economics Statistics, Inc., pointed out that the Dutch were members not only of the tin pool, but also of the Chadbourne Sugar Plan, the New Rubber Scheme and the Tea Restriction. Backman added, however, that the agitation for an investigation had arisen as the result of a sharp rise in tin prices. He wrote further:

"A careful analysis indicates that tin prices both in New York and in London have risen out of all proportion to the increase in consumption. . . . It is evident that the pool was more than successful in raising the price and, after having raised it, in maintaining it at a steady level."

Backman outlined the obstacles in the path of the pool's future operations, and he put his finger on some of the factors which were to contribute to Patiño's eventual difficult position. Production, he said, was not in the hands of the most efficient producers, and this fact would lead eventually to the splitting away of low-cost producers like the Malayans. Second, tin production in excess of export quotas, with the consequent accumulation of inventories among the Association's members, was a real danger because production could not be reduced sharply without increasing costs. Third, there was noted a slow but definite increase in production in the free areas. Fourth, a trend toward the use of substitute products wherever possible. Fifth, a much higher use of reclaimed tin. Sixth, the possibility of a consumer's strike.

The basic fallacy of the tin control plan, Backman declared, was its equal treatment of both high-cost and low-cost producers, a fallacy which would be aggravated by any future decline in world demand and a consequent downward revision of quotas.

Other factors began to affect Patiño's tin empire. By 1936 the combination of Bolivia's foreign exchange restrictions and the manpower shortage resulting from the Chaco War had cut into the little man's profits. The company's report for 1935 showed an income of 29,272 pounds after taxes, depreciation, depletion and other deductions. This did not include a 5 per cent reserve on mining profits, totaling 24,820 pounds, which Patiño charged against surplus. The 1935 profit was measured against 81,862 pounds which the company earned the previous year.

On the other hand, however, it was disclosed that Patiño had a sum of $13,444,252 which was not subject to Bolivian exchange restrictions, a sum made up of cash held by the tin king in London and New York, plus securities held by General Tin Industries, Inc., a wholly owned subsidiary. These securities were 400,000 pounds more than the total entered on General Tin's balance sheet.

In 1937, Patiño's report to the stockholders struck a gloomy note again. He declared that Bolivia's position as the world's second largest producer of tin was jeopardized by the labor shortage and the government's monetary policies. The mineral reserves of Patiño Mines, he said, had been depleted by more than 63,430 long tons in the past three years. Thus Patiño had to face a situation which he had helped materially to create by his activities in the Chaco War. And in spite of his foreboding words, the actual financial report showed a net profit of 100,360 pounds for 1936, a substantial recovery from the previous year.

When war came in 1939, the slowly accumulating storm over tin control broke, particularly as it dawned on the United States and British governments that the smelting situation created by Patiño had put the anti-Nazi countries in a perilous position. Edsel Kelly, writing in *The Nation* for November, 1940, analyzed the methods of monopoly capital by which affairs had been allowed to get into such a state. "Whether the United States can assure itself of an adequate tin supply depends upon its willingness and ability to break the tin monopoly," he wrote.

Kelly went on to depict the background of intrigue and negotiation against which Patiño played his attempted holdup drama. Kelly wrote:

"The handful of American firms which have the technical qualifications and the equipment to build and operate large tin smelters have been very cautious about tangling with the Patiño cartel. Even the bait of a government guaranty of profits has not tempted them. The State Department, looking at the international implications of the problem, wants the smelters to be government-owned. The tin specialists on the National Defense Commission, however, lean toward an arrangement with the National Lead Company, with which Patiño is closely connected. Two of these specialists are former employees of National Lead; another was formerly a Williams, Harvey salesman.

"Negotiations among the State Department, RFC Administrator Jesse Jones, the Bolivian government and Bolivian producers have been dragging on for months. Besides Patiño, who recently arrived from France, the "big three" of Bolivian tin include Mauricio Hochschild and Carlos Victor Aramayo. Hochschild, of German origin, is an Argentine citizen who has built up large interests in Bolivian tin during the past ten years. In 1936, 28.9 per cent of Bolivian tin exports came from his mines, as against 51 per cent from Patiño's. He would welcome any step that would break Patiño's grip on the international ore market. Aramayo, a former Minister to Great Britain, is the owner of the third largest mining corporation in Bolivia. He also is eager to get out of the cartel, as are the numerous smaller independent mine owners. As a result of the negotiations, an agreement has just been concluded by the Metal Reserve Company, a subsidiary of the Reconstruction Finance Corporation, with Hochschild, Aramayo and some lesser producers. The Metal Reserve Company has agreed to buy tin concentrates sufficient to smelt about 18,000 tons of tin annually for five years. It will either build a smelting plant of its own or contract with a private concern to smelt and refine the ore.

"It is highly significant that Patiño is not a party to this agreement. Whether he was actually edged out or stayed out voluntarily is a matter for speculation. It is probable that he will try to get in on the building of the smelters, for he must see the necessity for alternative processing plants in case Great Britain falls. For the moment, the new arrangement will in no way impair British interests. The Patiño mines are still under contract to Great Britain for ten years. Besides, the Metal Reserves Company has agreed to release to the British, if they want it, an additional 6,000 tons of Bolivian tin a year. . . .

"Ever since Patiño rose to power, Bolivia has been, in effect, a 'company town,' its economic and political development retarded by the overwhelming importance of tin. Living in Europe, with an income many times as large as the Bolivian national budget, Patiño has virtually ruled the country as an absentee landlord. So long as its tin can be smelted only in England, the country is dependent on Patiño, who has the power to dictate how much tin it is to export and therefore how much of other things it can import. Thinly populated as it is, it must import 75 per cent of its food supplies. Such dependence on one product is bad for any country, and disastrous for a small one. If a substitute for tin is ever found, or if the demand for tin drops after the war, Bolivia will face a serious situation. A market in the United States, however, would give the country a fairly large degree of economic independence and enable the government to regulate the industry according to the country's needs.

"Last year, shortly before his death, German Busch, the Bolivian dictator, attempted a bold move against Patiño. He issued a decree establishing state control of tin exports. But to make this decree effective smelters had to be established either in the United States or in Bolivia. Busch was unable to do either. His decree remained a dead letter, but it has never been repealed.

"The establishment of an American tin industry may not only solve a crucial problem of hemisphere defense but deliver Bolivia from feudal bondage."

But nearly a year later, Patiño was still hampering American moves to bolster this country's supply of tin, unwittingly or not, because all Patiño's tin was going to America's ally, Great Britain, and there was none left over for an increasingly desperate United States. An analysis of the situation as of August, 1941, prepared by the research division of Merrill Lynch, Pierce, Fenner and Beane, a New York Stock Exchange firm, indicates how the stage was set for Patiño's self-decapitation, as far as American interests were concerned. The report read:

"The tense political situation in the Far East, the principal source of tin supplies for the United States, has revived speculative activity in Patiño Mines. This interest is apparently based on the assumption that interference with tin shipments from the Far East would enable Patiño to market a substantial portion of its outfit profitably in the United States. However, our investigations indicate that Patiño is not participating now in furnishing any part of our tin requirements.

"We communicated with the management of Patiño in an effort to elicit from the company some comment on our findings but received only the following reply: 'We do not consider it appropriate to comment on your memorandum or to disclose our program otherwise than in due course to our stockholders.' The following statements are therefore without official standings.

"It is our understanding that Patiño Mines will not ship a single ton of tin concentrates for refining to the American tin smelter now under construction in Texas. Patiño has a ten-year contract with Consolidated Tin Smelters, Ltd. (in which Patiño has a substantial stock interest) to ship all of its concentrates to England. Obviously, if need for conserving shipping space across the Atlantic reaches a point where the bulk of Patiño's tin concentrates no longer can be shipped to England, the company will be seeking an outlet for it elsewhere.

"The American tin smelter, expected to be in operation early next year, is designed for processing Bolivian ores, which are all of relatively low grade. However, we understand that this ore will not come from the mines of Patiño but from other Bolivian producers. The Metals Reserve Company has a contract with the Bolivian Government which assures the American tin smelter a five-year supply of tin concentrates sufficient for capacity operation at the now-contemplated capacity of 18,000 tons of refined tin per annum. Furthermore, it was recently announced that the Metals Reserve Company made an agreement with Netherlands East Indies tin interests for the acquisition of tin concentrates containing

20,000 tons of fine tin. These high-grade concentrates are to be shipped to the new smelter for mixing with low-grade Bolivian material. In view of these facts it appears that Patiño does not enter the American tin smelting picture at the present time.

"As is indicated in the annual report of Patiño Mines for 1940, the company has organized a subsidiary in the state of Delaware, under the name of Smelters Development Corporation, in order to be in a position to smelt, in the United States, concentrates produced by Patiño and other Bolivian mines under the company's control. Obviously, such a step would have to be preceded by the construction of a tin smelter, and judging by the length of time required to build the Texas smelter, this may require anywhere from six to eighteen months, depending upon priorities.

"The shipment of Bolivian tin concentrates to the United States should build up dollar balances and thus improve the foreign exchange position of that country, but how much is an open question. Under regulations in effect last year, Patiño was obliged to deliver 42 per cent of its sterling drafts to the Bolivian Government at a rate which last year averaged 138 bolivianos per pound sterling. The company might liberalize its dividend payments if circumstances permit easing of Bolivian foreign exchange restrictions; this possibility is to our knowledge the only benefit in sight for the company, in connection with the tin situation.

"In the light of the foregoing, Patiño Mines common

stock is regarded as amply priced at current levels of about 10."

This report was in effect, and without intending to be, an obituary for Patiño interests in America. Between its lines can be read the story of how the little man's Bolivian competitors beat him to the punch in America's hour of need. The creation of Smelters Development Corporation was an effort to meet that competition and find an outlet for his tin ore. But he had delayed too long.

The story of how he brought himself to defeat is told in the pages which follow.

The first thing Simon Patiño did on his arrival last week was to try to get aboard the U. S. defense juggernaut. He told the press he is "entirely in accord" with hemisphere defense plans (which means he would sell all his ore to the U. S.), would help U. S. defense by building a $2,000,000 smelter here, would see the Defense Advisory Commission as soon as he caught his breath. But the Defense Commission, feeling tough, was in no hurry. It knew that ex-internationalist Patiño had nowhere else to go.—Time, *August 26, 1940.*

18

The Barons of Bolivia

ALL THE TIN barons of Bolivia have had their troubles with labor. In the case of at least one of Patiño's two major rivals, the troubles have been even greater than those of the little man. This one is Mauricio Hochschild, the fabulous operator whose acquisitive trail has crossed Patiño's more often than that of any other Bolivian tin man.

Hochschild controls four great Bolivian tin companies: Cía. Minera Unificada, operated from Buenos Aires; Cía. Minera de Cruro and Cía. Estanifera Morco-cala, operated from Chile; and Cía. de Minas de Colquiri, administered from Oruro, Bolivia. The first of these companies alone owns and operates twenty mines, producing 75 per cent of Hochschild tin.

In his extraordinary career, Hochschild has achieved several apparent miracles, the greatest of which is his ability to stay alive. The mysterious, baldish, heavy-faced giant of a man has lived much of his life in constant fear of execution, assassination or lynching by his starving workers. Once he was even under sentence of execution by the Bolivian government.

Nearly always Hochschild's Argentine citizenship has saved him. The United States has also intervened in his behalf, and the Chilean Ambassador, Benjamin Cohen, has come to plead for him as he lay in the La Paz jail. The Argentine diplomats are always on the alert to protect him.

Hochschild is hated by Bolivians for the same reason that Patiño is—because his policy has been to depress wages. He has been accused, both publicly and privately, of exploiting the country's resources of tin, tungsten, silver and zinc; his actual mineral holdings may even exceed Patiño's. His methods, which have always prevented diversification, have helped to create Bolivia's lopsided economy, with which there is nothing comparable in the world.

The balding giant was last arrested in 1944, when he was accused of plotting the overthrow of the newest *caudillo,* Gualberto Villaroel, many of whose followers were Jew-haters. With anti-Semitism at a new height, Bolivians were sure that Hochschild at last would have his oversized frame riddled with bullets. Instead, he was released from jail, only to be kidnaped later under the most mysterious circumstances. His automobile was found overturned near La Paz, and he disappeared for seventeen days. He reappeared in public and offered no explanation, saying blandly: "It has all been such a horrible mistake." To this day Hochschild has never disclosed the names of his abductors and has refused to give any reason for the kidnaping.

A few weeks after his release, he appeared in New York and announced that he was in America to ask the government to raise the price of his tin to 65 cents per pound. He held a press conference in his suite at the Ritz-Carlton Hotel, after breakfast one morning, and told the reporters in his oblique way what was on his mind. He observed that his cereal had come from Battle Creek, his eggs from Long Island, his ham from Virginia and his coffee from Brazil, and that the cigar which dropped ashes on his vest was a Brazilian product, while the purpose of the press conference, he added, was to talk about the situation of tin in Bolivia.

"All of these things," Hochschild remarked, "give our discussion an international flavor."

This was a subtle reference to the worldwide character of Patiño's tin empire, by which the more his tin travels under his control, the more money he makes. The object of Hochschild's visit was not only to get the price of tin raised, but to close a deal with the United States government and with private industrialists so that he could break Patiño's smelting monopoly. That monopoly had always compelled him to play second fiddle to Patiño.

Hochschild and Patiño were alike in at least two fundamental ways. They had both risen from poverty, Hochschild having once been a hobo, and both had always been single-minded on the subject of tin, no matter what else befell them. One fundamental difference was that Hochschild had always been a wanderer. Born in Beberach, Germany, he had studied in Freiberg to be a mining engineer, but soon became an ardent traveler. He knew the entire globe at first-hand. Everywhere he lived dangerously, but never more dangerously than in Bolivia, where he dabbled in that country's most fatal occupation—politics.

As he wound his devious way through Bolivian life, Hochschild had entertained politicians well, fed them huge, expensive meals, dined and plotted with every man of influence and power. His largess to Catholic charities was boundless, a popular activity in Catholic Bolivia. But he gave lavishly to refugee Jews as well as to nuns and priests. He laughed and joked with Bolivian army generals, while the smaller fry got his endless supply of cigars and paid for them by laughing at his repertoire of bad jokes. In all this, he was concerned only with the health of tin—his tin. A good government, to his way of thinking, was one that would help mine owners. Any other government was bad, and he watched the trends zealously.

"Bolivian labor," he once remarked, "strictly from a standpoint of efficiency, is the highest paid in the world. For the production of 40,000 tons of tin per year, we need 40,000 tons of men."

"Do you regard men, workers, in terms of tonnage?" someone asked.

"That, of course, is dynamite," he replied. "Don't say

that. You misunderstand me. I said 40,000 men, not 40,000 tons. You may say 40,000 men, if you wish."

That would mean, if true, that on the basis of present tin prices, Bolivian tin workers are being paid more than the value of the country's annual production.

The core of Hochschild's plan to break the Patiño monopoly lies in this statement he has made: "Bolivian tin concentrates do not have to be mixed with any others for proper smelting. The same type of myth once persisted as to copper. Until the end of the last century, it was an erroneously accepted 'fact' that England's Swansea was the only company with the copper 'know-how.' The United States later started experiments with this metal and today is the leading copper smelter of the world."

Will the same be true of tin? That is the question which keeps Patiño awake nights. If Hochschild's plans ever materialize and the United States does assume such smelting leadership, every electric light bulb switched on in an American home, and literally thousands of other vital articles, will be cut drastically in price. Everyone except Patiño will benefit.

American ingenuity already has accomplished many unheard-of things with tin. When the United States became panicky over shortages, even before the second World War, the government found some hope in the processes worked out successfully by the Metal & Thermite Company, and the Detinning Company, which together had recovered 10,000 tons of scrap from old tin cans and other tin products as long ago as 1926. That is another kind of development which makes Patiño shudder.

Some day American ingenuity may break Patiño's grip on smelting entirely, may disprove the old cry that foreign metallurgists are the only ones who can refine the silvery ore, and that high labor costs here make competition with foreign companies unprofitable. If the worldwide travels of tin under Patiño's plan are ever curtailed, it may well be the answer to the differential involved. A nation like America, which can make and discard 25 tons of tinned tooth paste and shaving cream tubes every day, is almost certain eventually to work the magic necessary to overcome any obstacles to domestic tin smelting.

In his Ritz-Carlton interview, Hochschild discussed these matters either directly or indirectly. He did not discuss Bolivian reports that he had organized a united front of Bolivian mine owners to block wage increases for miners from 6.60 bolivianos, or fifteen cents per day average pay, even with 10,000 men and women out on strike. He shook his head nervously when the reporters asked him about the arrest of union organizers, and about his opposition to a Patiño agreement to raise wages 30 per cent, unless the Penaranda government would abolish the labor code designed to improve the lot of the workers. Nor did he have anything to say about charges that he, a Jew, was an employer of notorious Nazis.

But when his first American interview was over,

Hochschild had succeeded in leaving the impression that he might be the man to revolutionize the world tin industry, and to give the United States its first permanent tin-smelting business. That would mean the lowest tin prices in scores of years for American tin users, who are far and away the world's greatest consumers of tin. Before the second World War, United States tinplate makers, automobile plants, paint factories and pewter works used about 87,000 tons a year—almost four times as much as the next largest consumer, the United Kingdom, and amounting to a third or a half of the total world consumption.

Patiño's particular advantage in this situation came from his ownership or part ownership of the world's big tin smelters, and from the long distances his tin has to travel. Bolivian ore had to be shipped down the Andes to Chilean ports, then up through the South Pacific, via the Panama Canal, and out through the Caribbean and the North Atlantic to Patiño-owned English smelters. After that, it came back over to New York, thus increasing the price satisfactorily for Patiño and keeping his British smelters busy. For the consumer, however, this arrangement was out of all proportion to what common sense told him he should be paying for tin.

Until Hochschild indicated that he might be able to do it, there appeared to be no way of breaking Patiño's smelting monopoly and of shortening his ore's long travels. Smelters in Bolivia failed because of the fuel lack and the strange refractory nature of the ore, which requires concentration as mined. Electric furnace methods were tried in Bolivia and elsewhere, but they were uniformly unsuccessful.

To make matters worse for the consumer and more profitable for the little man, Patiño also asserted that his tin ore was of such low grade that it required mixing with the rich cassiterides of Malaya. This "necessity" brought into the monopoly picture all of Patiño's Far Eastern holdings, including mines in Siam and Borneo, and a big smelter in Penang.

In short, no matter where tin originated, it came to the United States only after long trips to cartel-owned smelters. "This," said Hochschild, "is not in the interest of the United States, to have tin travel so much."

The war and Hochschild have made the first dent in Patiño's monopoly. When the Japs cut off Far Eastern mines and smelters, the United States looked frantically for a new and closer source of refined tin. At the suggestion of Hochschild, an American-financed, Dutch-built and operated smelter was erected at Texas City, Texas. By 1945, it was operating at a capacity of between 30,000 and 75,000 tons annually. Except for a Brooklyn smelter built and abandoned promptly thereafter by Patiño in the first World War, this is the first big smelter to operate in the United States. American Smelting and Phelps-Dodge operate pilot plants.

When he came to the United States, Hochschild's intent was to convince United States tin consumers that the smelter should be operated permanently, not junked like the one built during the last war. If he succeeds, Hochschild then hopes to sign a contract whereby the United States will take all the tin he can produce—15,000 to 25,000 tons annually. Should this occur, the Argentinian-Bolivian-world citizen will be completely free of his arch-rival, Simon Patiño.

To put the deal across, Hochschild has some telling arguments. The combination of United States smelting and Hochschild tin would make the United States at least semi-independent of the tin cartel. Prices would come down sharply because tin would travel directly from South America to North America. With some of the money saved in transportation, Hochschild says he wants to help the Bolivian tin miners—a voluntary gesture unprecedented in his career. He could also profitably spend millions in improving Bolivian mining equipment, which is so outmoded that it takes 40,000 Bolivians to produce 40,000 tons of tin a year.

Even if Hochschild's plans are successful, however, it does not mean that the hold of Patiño and the Committee will be entirely broken. The United States could obtain enough non-Patiño tin to supply its needs, but all manufacturers would not be able to buy American production. Many large tin users are bound by contract to use Patiño tin from Patiño smelters. The National Lead Company, for example, uses Patiño tin almost exclusively.

As matters stand now, Patiño still remains firmly at the top of the tin heap. His nearest rival in Bolivian production is charming, Oxford-educated Don Carlos Aramayo, the only aristocrat in the country's tin industry. Aramayo owns four mines south of Potosí—Tasna, Chorolque, Caracoles and Animas, all capitalized at 20,-000,000 Swiss francs and operated from Geneva.

But Patiño dwarfs them all. He came first, he stayed, and he made even the success of his rivals possible. Only 14,000 long tons of tin had been mined in Bolivia when Patiño and Albina hit upon their Salvadora vein. Since that time, Patiño's methods and enterprise have made it possible to mine 1,000,000 long tons in fifty-four years—about one-sixth of total world production since 1801, when accurate statistics were first compiled.

Shortly after Pearl Harbor, a South American newspaper carried an eloquent editorial summary of Patiño's position as the czar of tin. The editorial declared:

"It is doubtful that any man in history, with the possible exception of Solomon, ever attained the great wealth of chubby little Simon Iturri Patiño. And all of it came from tin.

"As this is written, the only tin in the world not Jap-seized is obtainable for the Allies in small quantities from Australia, uncertain tonnage out of the tropical hell of Nigeria, specks from California, negligible pounds from Alaska, niggardly bits from Nigger Hill in South Dakota.

"Queen Wilhelmina's chemically pure ore in her islands near Bali, the mines in China's Yunnan hills, the Malay States and the smelter of Singapore near Britain's impregnable $45,000,000 naval base, and the tin of the teeth-sucking little monkey men of the bespectacled simpering son of hell.

"All? Not quite! Patiño still has in his deep mines in the Andes, worked by silicosis-stricken, drug-addicted Indians, enough unshackled tin safe from the Nipponese to supply the most urgent needs of the warring world. As usual, Patiño in 1940 was sitting pretty."

Five years later Patiño is still at the top, but his position is not as secure. The reopening of the Far East, perhaps under greatly changed political conditions, plus whatever changes in the international cartel that peace may bring, plus the potential future of American smelting—all these things may mean that the aged Patiño will die in the deep twilight of the fabulous empire he created.

PANAMA, R. P., May 9.—Simon Patiño, Bolivian tin magnate, divided and bequeathed to his heirs one of the world's largest fortunes in instruments signed and registered before a notary public here yesterday. The total value of properties involved was not revealed.

Patiño and wife, here en route to the United States, distributed all their estate except their home in Paris, their villa at Biarritz, two houses at Oruro, Bolivia, and 30,000 shares of the electric light and power company of Cochabamba, Bolivia, which were left to the Patiño University Foundation. The estate goes to their son, Antenor Patiño, and his wife, Cristina Bourbon de Patiño; Doña Graziela Patiño de Ortiz-Linares; Doña Elena Patiño de Garrisosa, wife of Jorge Lopez Garrisosa, Marques del Merito; Doña Luzmila Patiño de Boisrouvray; and Rene Patiño. All will enter upon immediate possession of their inheritances except Rene Patiño, whose share is held in trust by his parents.—New York Times, *May 10, 1941.*

19

"Albina! Albina!"

PATIÑO'S ACTIVITIES in the second World War foreshadowed the twilight of his world. They made him wealthier, but at the same time, the handwriting began to form on the wall.

In the early days of the war, Patiño was in a constant state of agitated travel. He dashed from occupied France to Vichy to London to Panama to Spain, and to many other countries which he did not choose to name. His problems were how to keep England from bombing his German smelters, Germany from bombing his Liverpool smelters, the British from bombing his Japanese-held Malaya smelters, and the Nazis in his own Bolivia from sabotaging his mines to prevent tin concentrates from reaching England.

These activities got him a bad press. One story charged, and he denied it, that he had backed Franco's regime, even in its earliest stages. Another, which he did not deny, concerned his intimacy with Mussolini. A third, which worried him greatly, was that he had actually dangled his metal in front of Hitler's eyes, and then dangled it elsewhere to scare the Fuehrer out of the idea of bombing his English smelters. A prominent American magazine charged that he tried to give the American government the jitters by consorting with the Nazis, but that the government failed to jitter.

Even while he squirmed under the lash, Patiño knew that his travels and associations would be profitable. His remarkable insight into such things told him that Germany could not win the war, even in the dark days of 1940, and consequently in that year he decided to visit the United States.

He sailed from Lisbon, and arrived at Jersey City on the American Export liner *Excambion.* The reporters were waiting for him. Patiño's previous uncertainty about the outcome of the war and his mysterious travels had been widely publicized long before his arrival. Thoroughly frightened by his reception, Patiño fled half the length of the ship while the reporters shouted questions after him: "Are you pro-Nazi? Did you finance Franco? Is your La Paz newspaper full of pro-Hitler propaganda?"

To these questions, Patiño's only reply was a frantic screaming of the name he had called so often in his life: "Albina!" His voice was a high shriek by this time.

"I do not speak English," he pleaded. "I do not speak English, I say."

"You're speaking it now," one reporter reminded him.

"Albina!" Patiño yelled again.

And suddenly Albina appeared. She shepherded her husband into a companionway and stood between him and the newspapermen. Bracing herself against the walls of the corridor, she barred their way until Patiño had reached the safety of his suite.

"My husband is ill," she said in Spanish.

None of the reporters spoke Spanish, but one understood what she said. There were attempts at conversation in German, then in French, until at last a reporter arrived who spoke fluent Spanish and took over the questioning.

"What about the Nazi domination of Bolivia?" he asked.

Albina looked at him blankly. The reporter amplified.

"Nazis in Bolivia are spending $40,000 monthly to spread anti-American propaganda in your country," he said. "Newspapers in La Paz are subsidized by the Nazis. Your husband owns one and he must know about this activity."

Albina's face remained expressionless. Once she looked toward her husband's suite, where he stood trembling within earshot, as though she half expected him to answer. But no word came and Albina did not speak.

The reporters persisted, asking questions through their interpreter, but Albina was adamant. She answered none of them.

"Has any of your husband's tin been offered to the Nazis?" the Spanish-speaking reporter tried once more.

Albina made no comment. The one-sided interview ended.

Patiño left his stateroom only after the vessel had berthed, and then not until he was surrounded by servants, members of his family, and Bolivian diplomats and business associates who had boarded the ship to greet him. The little man showed no signs of illness as he raced down the gangplank, and sprinted across the dock to a limousine which whisked him off to his quarters in the Waldorf-Astoria. Albina rode beside him. The others in his entourage brought up the rear in a cavalcade of chauffeured Cadillacs and Packards, an imposing procession. The reporters trailed along in taxis. Their city desks had told them to keep after the little man.

Meanwhile, the news of Patiño's reception at the Jersey City pier had reached his American executives in their 20 Exchange Place offices, and it disturbed them. The old man had never before been so pressed to answer questions, and the questions had never been so embarrassing. Hitherto, and in other countries, Patiño had simply brushed the press aside. This was his first real experience with the American press. Up to now he had never been interviewed by a working newspaperman. He had successfully immured himself behind a wall of mystery.

When Patiño settled himself at the Waldorf, his executives told him bluntly: "This is serious. These pro-Nazi stories won't die down." The old man's son Antenor agreed, and so did his son-in-law, Ortiz-Linares, a director of his company. Further argument on the same line came from representatives of the Bolivian Embassy and of National Lead.

Both Patiño and Albina listened to these worried comments, which culminated in the suggestion that Patiño grant a mass interview. His advisers pointed out that he had nowhere else to come with his tin except the United States, since Nazi submarines threatened every ton of his ore that was shipped to England. It was entirely conceivable, they reminded him, that the blockade would put his one remaining smelter out of business, or curtail its production so that new riots would break out among his miners.

For the first time in his life, Patiño needed Yankee good will, the "understanding" of Americans, and a good press. If the Germans bombed the Liverpool smelter and at the same time prevented ships from traveling between South America and England, Patiño's tin empire would temporarily cease to function. His one hope, in such a case, would be a tin smelter in the United States, closer to the Bolivian mines and relatively safe from submarines. On the other hand, if he did build a United States smelter, it would be necessary to work out a compromise with the British tin monopoly. He could send enough of his ore to America to make his mining operations profitable, then junk the smelter, as he had done after the previous war, and thus keep his world monopoly intact. Patiño knew that Hochschild was also in the United States, and he suspected that his old enemy also had plans for an American smelter, with all that would mean to his control of tin in Bolivia.

With these things in mind, Patiño conferred briefly with Albina and announced: "I'll see the reporters—here, now, today. Bring them in."

As he waited for the newspapermen to come up, Patiño might have been in an even more unsettled frame of mind if he had read the newspaper and magazine comments which had already greeted his arrival. *Time* had asserted bluntly that Patiño came to America simply "because he had no other place to go." Newspapers described him as "ruthless" and "cunning." The New York *World-Telegram* had revived the old charge that Patiño, through his investments in the French munitions firm of Schneider-Creusot, had profited during the Chaco War by sales of arms to both Paraguay and Bolivia. *Coronet Magazine* pictured Patiño as an unscrupulous titan, greedy and selfish, and in fact tarred him with so black a brush that it later had to retract. Other publications asserted that "all Bolivia" was a "Patiño company town."

The Nation was more blunt than the others in its article by Edsel Kelly, already quoted in part. It declared:

". . . Bolivian Nazis have not been idle. A Bolivian fifth column is putting pressure on the government to sabotage the Washington [tin] negotiations. If victorious, Germany will go to any length to wrest control of the Bolivian tin industry from the United States. Patiño, whose leanings toward the Axis are well known, is an important factor in the German calculations. His chief supporters in Bolivia belong to Nazi circles—pro-Nazi army officers and influential Nazi agents. He is hated by the Bolivian masses and any deal made with him by the United States would add fuel to the feeling against American imperialism."

Patiño's advisers, who had read such comments, knew that the only way to meet them was for the tin king to make his answers publicly in a press conference. They knew, and Patiño knew, that it was even more important to establish the Patiño case in the United States against the inroads of Hochschild, and of Aramayo, who was also in America.

When the press at last confronted Patiño, he insisted that the interview be conducted in Spanish, although he could speak both English and French. That would give him time to think, to feint and spar a little. His son-in-law served as interpreter, and his shrewd son Antenor stood at his side to interrupt if the going became rough. Albina listened from another room, sitting near a door left ajar.

Albina knew what her husband would say, even though she had her fearful doubts of what the reporters might ask. She hoped that history would repeat itself, that Patiño would again be commissioned to build a smelter in America which he could conveniently dismantle at the end of the war. Albina approved of the interview because she thought it would prime the American public, get Patiño on record as willing and anxious to help the United States, forestall Hochschild, and impress Washington so that his forthcoming conferences there would be easier. Albina listened eagerly for every word.

The reporters, for their part, hoped to smell out Patiño and get into a news story what had hitherto been mostly editorial and columnar speculation.

A reporter from the New York *Mirror* almost immediately asked the question Patiño wished to be asked. "Mr. Patiño," he inquired, "is it true that you are pro-Nazi and would block the building of a United States tin smelter?"

Patiño glanced toward Ortiz-Linares, and the interpreter repeated the query, to which of course Patiño had already framed his reply.

"Block it?" Patiño answered. "Why, I'm here to help build a smelter. It is just the contrary. During the first World War, I constructed a smelter in Brooklyn. I am a friend in need to the United States."

"What is your attitude toward the Allies?" a *Times* man asked.

"I am entirely in accord with President Roosevelt's program for hemisphere defense," Patiño responded, "and I will cooperate to the utmost to help make it effective. As to my alleged Nazi leanings, how can I have any? My holdings in England should be sufficient to show the falsity of such a charge. It is ridiculous. Furthermore, there is no great increase of Nazi influence in Bolivia."

"Are you one of the richest men in the world?" another reporter asked.

Patiño appeared amused when his son-in-law translated this question. His tone was almost sarcastic when he replied: "I am not privileged to be a citizen of this country, and hence was unable to make such a huge fortune as a citizen of this country seems able to make. My fortune is large, but not large by comparison with some."

A reporter asked Patiño his age.

"My age?" he inquired, in a pained manner. "I am as old as I look. Like my wealth, this is grossly exaggerated. I am only concerned now with helping the United States in its tin problems. I will offer my assistance, technical and otherwise, in the construction of a smelter."

With that, the interview ended.

Before Patiño left for Washington that night, he read the stories in the afternoon papers and was satisfied. He had been pictured exactly as he wished, and he decided on the spot to impress the nation further with his loyalty by holding another interview in Washington and reiterating what he had said in New York. So delighted was he with the way his first interview had been handled, that his aides were amazed to discover the hermit Patiño had turned into a publicity seeker.

The second interview was held in Patiño's suite at the Mayflower Hotel in Washington, and the routine of the first meeting was repeated in detail. The reporters asked the proper questions and the newspapers conveyed exactly what he wanted to convey. Mrs. Patterson's *Times-Herald*, which might have been friendly to Patiño in any event, reported:

"In an atmosphere of mystery, behind closed doors in his suite at the Mayflower, Simon Patiño, the tin king, one of the world's least-known super-multimillionaires, yesterday outlined a plan for bringing a tin smelter to the United States."

All the papers quoted the statement Patiño most wanted quoted: "I wish to cooperate with the government in every way."

As he read these stories, Patiño smiled confidently and prepared for his State Department interview. Antenor and Ernest Pearce, general manager of the Consolidated English Smelters, were also to be at this momentous meeting.

As Patiño emerged from the elevator on the Mayflower's lobby floor, en route to the consummation of his efforts, an aide hurried to him, holding a newspaper in his hand.

"Mr. Patiño, you will wish to read this!" he said.

Patiño read, looked up blankly, and said to Antenor: "I am too late. Hochschild has beaten me to it. Phone Albina in her room."

He found his way to a chair and sat down limply, while Antenor hurried to call Albina. Meanwhile, Pearce read the newspaper report with obvious agitation.

At the telephone, Antenor was saying: "Hochschild is in Washington with Dutch engineers. He will build the smelter! What shall we do?"

"Keep your appointment," Albina told him. "Keep your appointment."

The appointment was kept, but Patiño knew at once that the situation was adverse. The State Department gentlemen were civil enough, but he observed that they were not enthusiastic. For once in his life, men who needed tin were not in a hurry to get his metal. While he had been wavering in Panama and Vichy and Madrid, Hochschild had been busy. Patiño left the meeting in a daze. Nothing had been settled.

When he returned to the Mayflower, a reporter approached him in the lobby and asked in English: "What is the status of the smelter, Mr. Patiño?"

The tin king was so upset that he thoughtlessly replied in the same language: "My personal opinion is that negotiations will be carried on."

But it was obvious that Patiño had lost, and the fact was underlined that night when Jesse Jones, RFC head, told reporters that "there are a great many knotty matters to be considered."

Next morning Patiño and his family left Washington for New York. The little man has never returned to the nation's capital. As the train rolled up through the Maryland meadows Patiño's bitter, anxious mood was not improved when he noted that Albina, for the first time since he had known her, appeared to be worried and strained.

Albina's confidence had been shaken by the failure of the men she had counted on most to make matters come out properly for her husband. These men, tin specialists on the National Defense Commission, all had been publicly advocating an "arrangement" with the Patiño-dominated National Lead Company. One of the specialists was a former salesman for the Williams, Harvey organization, likewise Patiño-controlled. The two others were ex-employees of National Lead. All of them together had not been able to control the powerful forces working against Patiño. Albina had been badly fooled.

When the Patiños got back to New York, they were staggered by still another blow of a different kind. Princess Cristina had instituted sealed divorce proceedings against Antenor in the New York courts, where the only grounds for such action is adultery. The woman who had brought Patiño his most exquisite social triumph now threatened to disgrace him at the worst possible moment.

Albina took charge of this new crisis and at once began a campaign to effect a reconciliation. It was a job that took all her special qualities of tact, force and diplomacy. While Patiño fretted at the Waldorf, Albina hurried back and forth between Antenor's quarters in the Hotel Plaza and Cristina's bower in the neighboring elegance of the Sherry-Netherlands, where she had moved when she first suspected her husband of infidelity.

Albina did her job well. Before the newspapers could print even a rumor of the scandalous proceedings, Cristina withdrew her action. It was a major victory. Patiño's servants heard him mutter a fervent "Thank God," when Albina telephoned him the news.

But the little man's woes were far from an end. Disastrous reports arrived daily from Bolivia. There was a new reign of terror, and friends of the deposed President Peneranda were being executed wholesale. Every Latin-American nation except Argentina was protesting this heedless slaughter by President Villaroel's butchers, and it was rumored that Washington would also protest to the Bolivian government.

While Patiño was still digesting these reports, there were legal actions brought against Cristina by a detective agency which had helped her get evidence for divorce proceedings and now claimed that its fee of many thousands of dollars had not been paid.

Further, as time went on, there were reports from Texas that the Hochschild smelter project was doing well, and more reports came from Bolivia of new labor strife and threatened civil war. Patiño's hands trembled as he read, day after day, the continued flow of bad news. For once Albina was no help. She sat staring out the window, and his old cry of "Albina!" brought only a listless "Yes, Simon," in reply.

If Patiño had been able to think of his situation impartially, as the closing years of the war and of his life began to draw a dark curtain around him, he would have seen that it was only just retribution long delayed. It was particularly ironic that this retribution should have come so soon after the little man had virtually forced it upon himself.

The crisis of Patiño's life, had he only known it, came in January, 1943, at a particularly delicate stage in United States-Bolivian relations. Bolivia itself presented a somewhat strange picture at the time, with American lend-lease jeeps hopping around the Andes, and Bolivian soldiers learning to march West Point style and to shoot with Garands, after their previous intensive training in the goose-step and the operation of Lugers. Now they wore lend-lease holsters, which held lend-lease automatics, and fired lend-lease bullets. American lend-lease planes frightened the condors. The United States was at war with Germany, and all the tin available in the world that could help America win the war was in Bolivia, a nation also at war with Germany.

In its efforts to get Bolivia's tin, the American government had made a deal with every tin miner except Patiño to purchase at a fancy price 18,000 tons every year for five years, at a cost of $87,000,000, or fifty cents per pound. The United States had flattered Bolivia in every possible way. It had signed a $25,000,000 Bolivian development program agreement, and set up a $10,000,000 Import-Export Bank credit for the country, although Bolivia was still in default on debts to America of $58,000,000.

At the moment Bolivian tin seemed almost as valuable as gold, but America had to have it at any price. Tin was essential to victory. Patiño's tin was apparently out of the question, because all of it went directly to Great Britain under a ten-year contract with Consolidated Tin Smelters, Ltd., which he owned. In 1943, tin was not as high as it was in the first World War, when it rocketed to $1.10 per pound, but it was 500 per cent higher than its lowest point in 1922, when it was worth only ten cents per pound.

When Japan attacked Pearl Harbor, the United States had a stockpile of tin so low that it made the knees of strong industrialists shake when they found out how low it was. The supply was estimated by the gloomiest at two weeks, by the most optimistic at two years. In any event, it was a major crisis.

The man who could have solved the problem almost instantly was Simon Iturri Patiño, the man who fraternized with Nazis up to the beginning of the war, who was an alleged backer and at the least an admirer of the Fascist Franco.

It was Patiño's fatal defect of character that cost him his great chance. The defect was his opportunism, which always had been an asset before. But opportunism this time made him waver, compelled him to hesitate until he was sure what course would be best for Patiño. The war did not hesitate, and America couldn't wait. Hochschild, no matter what his motives, had already come forward with his plan to smelt tin in the United States, and to supply that smelter with Hochschild tin. Patiño might have recaptured both his political and financial prestige if he had turned the immense power of his empire toward winning the war for America and her allies, including Bolivia.

But in the moment of crisis, Patiño thought only of how his power could be utilized for the acquisition of more power and the stifling of his competitors. It was a different kind of opportunism than Hochschild's. It was a kind that might have done very well, and had indeed done handsomely, in the old days, but it was completely overwhelmed in the gigantic upheaval of World War II.

As he retreated into his Waldorf-Astoria fastness after the rebuff in Washington, Patiño must have realized that he had come to the end of his career. He would still be an immensely wealthy man in the years left to him, no matter what happened, but the fabulous days of supreme wealth and influence were over.

Patiño was a rich old man—rich and forgotten.

Operating prospects for Patiño Mines & Enterprises are obscured by reports that large producers of tin in Bolivia are encountering ores of decreasing grade. Lower exports are therefore anticipated during the balance of 1943, especially since shipments earlier in the year were aided by large quantities of accumulated concentrates resulting from 1942 mining. . . .—From a Wall Street financial report—October 11, 1943.

20

The Road to a Blue Marble Tomb

A PORTRAIT of Patiño in these latter days of his life can be drawn only from gossip and from newspaper accounts of his numerous litigations. The portrait is one of a king in eclipse, an aged hermit counting his gold, a man who is spending his last days in loneliness and isolation, except when he is called to account for some past sin, real or imaginary.

All wealthy men are constantly involved with the law, inasmuch as money and sex are the prime movers in legal matters as they are in other forms of human relations. But Patiño's court appearances, or in most cases non-appearances, have been peculiarly embarrassing. He is seldom involved in a dull suit involving bookkeeping or complex financial matters designed to keep him off the front pages. The suits brought against him are almost invariably full of scandal, and calculated to make him lose face no matter what happens.

Perhaps his most bitter recent experience, and one that he could not forget, was the $100,000 suit charging assault and slander brought before the New York Supreme Court in 1942 by Mrs. Aimee Appiato Musich, a former lady's maid to Mrs. Patiño.

A jury of eleven men and a woman listened to the strange proceedings in this litigation for several days, and in less than an hour returned a verdict awarding Mrs. Musich $6,000 for alleged beating and abuse at the hands of both Patiños in the presence of several Waldorf-Astoria employees. Neither Patiño nor his wife appeared in court to defend themselves against the charges brought by the frail thirty-seven-year-old woman. They were represented by an attorney who asked the jury to consider the "volatile Latin temperaments" of the three principals. Mrs. Musich herself was a Parisian.

The Appellate Division unanimously reversed the Supreme Court jury's verdict and ordered a new trial unless the plaintiff agreed to reduce the judgment to $2,181, but the legal double-talk boiled down to an upholding, in effect, of the basis of Mrs. Musich's charges. The Patiños entered no defense against the maid's action.

Mrs. Musich had been in the service of many noted employers, including Marion Davies; Lady Deterding, widow of Sir Henry Deterding, former head of the Royal Dutch Petroleum Company; and Denis Conan Doyle, Sir Arthur's son, and his wife, the former Princess Nina

Mdivani. Both the latter appeared in court as character witnesses.

The plaintiff's laborious testimony was the story of an altercation on the thirty-fourth floor of the Waldorf, where the Patiños lived in a fourteen-room suite. The quarrel was no noisy that the screams and imprecations were heard all over that wing of the hotel, attracting the attention of house detectives and an assistant manager, all of whom came on the run to stop what everyone thought was a murder.

"They hit me every place they could," the maid testified. "Then they broke my dress. Then Mrs. Patiño took the key and opened the door, all of us fighting for my purse. Madame, she was screaming, '*Tu as volé ma montre!*' which means in French that I stole her watch, and Monsieur, he called me bad words in Spanish. Then I left. After that, I was dizzy and weak. I couldn't sleep or eat for a long time."

All of this occurred, Mrs. Musich testified, because she had given notice to the Patiños that she intended to leave their employ, which she did later in Panama.

"Mrs. Patiño gave me a dollar and a half a day to eat on in Panama," she testified, "and everything was very expensive there, so that wasn't enough."

The witness' testimony produced a graphic description of the Battle of the Waldorf. According to Mrs. Musich, she found Mrs. Patiño and the master himself in her room in the servants' section of the suite. Mrs. Patiño was searching the drawers of her bureau, she said.

"I asked them what was going on," Mrs. Musich whispered on the stand. "Madame then charged me with stealing the watch, one which I had never seen. My room was ransacked. The police I offer to call, but Monsieur, he say this not necessary since he have police power as a Bolivian diplomat. Madame she then take my handbag from the drawer and try to leave room. I lock door to stop her and then telephone police."

At that point, according to the testimony, all hell broke loose and there was such a bedlam of scuffling and screaming that the maids from the floors above and below gathered outside the room.

It was all very embarrassing, said Mrs. Musich, an incident which injured her health permanently and caused her great humiliation and serious results to her nervous system.

Patiño did not emerge from this trial as a figure of dignity. The newspapers could scarcely let anyone forget the story that the richest man in the world gave a lady's maid $1.50 a day for three meals.

In June, 1945, Patiño was in the courts under even more humiliating personal circumstances. This time the plaintiff was a pretty twenty-five-year-old French brunette named Suzanne Auclert Roth, identified as Patiño's godchild. When the suit was first filed in May, the New York *Daily News* greeted it joyfully with the headline: TIN GOLD FLOW STOPS, SO BABY SUES PATIÑO. In its own inimitable fashion, the *News* went on to say:

Señor Simon I. Patiño, reputed to have almost as many millions as his Bolivian tin mines have produced plates, is in the wringer. Winding the crank is one Suzanne Auclert Roth, a right pert little wren of 25, who says the old boy—he's 80 or better—is her godfather and ain't been doing right by her.

Señor Patiño, says this Suzanne, promised in 1940 to pay her $1,000 a month if she'd blow her native Paris and come to America and sing for him. She also was to consider him her old man, says the suit she filed agin the señor in Manhattan Supreme Court yesterday.

"However," allows Mlle. Roth, in effect, "he ain't paid me for 35 months, so I now demand 35 grand and a promise that he'll keep pitching until I have no more natural life left, like he said he would."

Suzanne's complaint, which wanders all over the lot before it gets down to business, asserts that she was born in 1920 in gay Paree, and that Patiño, then Bolivian minister to France, stood up for her. She always called him "Uncle" after that, she says.

In 1940 Patiño came to New York and moved into the Waldorf Towers, Suzanne goes on. And it was then that he urged her to come to these United States on a visitor's visa and be his constant and devoted companion. For that, she asserts, he promised to pay her $1,000.

But in October of that year her visa ran out and Patiño, according to Mlle. Roth, sent her to Montreal so she could reenter the country on a permanent visa. To enable her to do so, she charges, Patiño entered into an agreement with the U. S. immigration authorities to support her to the tune of $1,000 a month.

Come May, 1942, and according to Suzanne, Si quit paying off. So she's suing. . . .

It developed later, in a bill of particulars, that Suzanne wanted $500,000, a figure based on $1,000 a month for the rest of her life, according to mortality tables. For this sum, she said, she had contracted to be at Patiño's beck and call during all her waking moments, as long as "none of the foregoing was inconsistent with my relationship with my husband." The husband was Georges J. Roth, whom she married in 1939, and who committed suicide in 1944.

Patiño, in a motion for dismissal, contended that the agreement was contrary to both "public policy" and "human nature." As the *News* so deftly put it: "Against public policy, they say, because Suzanne was admittedly married to another man. And against human nature, they say, because none is so 'rugged' that he 'can remain unaffected by the fact that a wife spends 16 hours a day (eight off for slumber) at the beck and call of another married man.' "

Even when Justice Benjamin F. Schreiber agreed with Patiño and dismissed the suit, the tin king could get little consolation out of such headlines as PATINO'S GAL GETS KICK IN THE PUSS. Few readers bothered to absorb Justice Schreiber's outraged legal opinion, which admitted there might not be anything meritricious involved, "but even thus credulously viewed, the agreement offends deep-rooted principles of morality and public policy. . . . The agreement is so directly and completely inconsistent with and destructive of plaintiff's marriage and defendant's as well, as to be utterly void in our system of morals."